THE VERY BEST OF
Billy Keane

THE VERY BEST OF
Billy Keane

A New Collection of
Weekly Columns

Ballpoint Press

Published in 2019 by Ballpoint Press
4 Wyndham Park, Bray,
Co Wicklow, Republic of Ireland.

Telephone: 00353 86 821 7631
Email: ballpointpress1@gmail.com
Web: www.ballpointpress.ie

ISBN 978-1-9160863-0-2

Cover photograph by Don MacMonagle

While every effort has been made to ensure the accuracy
of all information contained in this book, neither the author nor
the publisher accept liability for any errors or omissions made.

Book design and production by Joe Coyle Media&Design,
joecoyledesign@gmail.com

Printed and bound by GraphyCems

Contents

CONTENTS

Introduction

FOR close on two decades, Listowel native Billy Keane has been the *Irish Independent*'s observer in and around middle Ireland.

The Kerry publican has used his base as a touchstone to measure changes and how Irish people react to different challenges as part of modern-day living.

Keane is a writer fearlessly on the side of the underprivileged and downtrodden and his courage in tackling taboo subjects has helped society throw a more sympathetic light on issues where once a hard focus was the order of the day.

Married with four adult children, Billy is the author of two novels, *The Last Of The Heroes* (2005) and *The Ballad of Mo & G* (2013).

He has also co-written the late Moss Keane's autobiography, *Rucks, Mauls and Gaelic Football* and Billy Morgan's autobiography *'Rebel, Rebel'*.

His first collection of columns, *The Best Of Billy Keane*, was published in 2017.

*Dad is 90 today – or 270,
seeing as he made three days
out of every birthday. I use
the word 'is' deliberately
because he is still with us,
even though if I was to get
technical, Dad is dead.*

1

Thoughts Of My Father Who'd Be 90 Today

July 21, 2018

I SIT on my own in the pub, among the old ghosts, thinking of happy birthdays past. He's there. He has to be. Dad would never leave me. He promised when I was eight.

Dad loved his birthdays. There was the day of, the day before, and the day after. He celebrated every one like it was his last. Dad was like a child when it came to the birthdays. And that was why he enjoyed every single one. He never sent away the small boy within.

Dad is 90 today — or 270, seeing as he made three days out of every birthday. I use the word 'is' deliberately because he is still with us, even though if I was to get technical, Dad is dead. Just reading those words, 'Dad is dead', comes as a shock, even now, 16 years on from when his body gave out.

So why the is? There are times when the customers are all gone home and I'm alone in the bar. The lights are down and the pub seems to go back in time. The songwriter Mickey MacConnell described the late-night John B's as "a silent, darkened stage".

Not only did I inherit a pub but dad also bequeathed unto me his thirst. I sit on my own then, drinking a vicarious pint, there among the old ghosts, thinking of happy birthdays past. He's there. He has to be. Dad would never leave me. He promised when I was eight.

It was my first day in Croke Park. Small ones always remember their first day in Croke Park and dad told me he would always be there for me. I believed him then and I believe him now.

I tell him my problems and my worries and just the other night, I imagined him saying to me: "Thing-a-nothing, Bill boy." Everything was "a thing-a-nothing".

I'm a terrible worrier and it has been worse than usual lately. It's only lately those words, 'a thing-a-nothing', came back in the late night reverie of Dad's spiritual repartee. I see his face in my mind. Kind and concerned, loving and understanding. He knew me. Dad left life clues for me all along the way up until the day he died.

From decades ago came his just-before-bed words, as I was good-nighting my own son John, who was heading off for the summer. Dad always said: "Good night sweet prince and may flights of angels guard thy repose." I'm sleeping a lot better since.

I suppose what I miss most about Dad are the jokes. He really was a stand-up dad. Here's one of my favourites and I may well have told it here before.

Mam was always at him about keeping his weight down. So one day she unilaterally withdrew the chocolate digestives Dad used to devour in large quantities after his dinner.

Dad was a dunker and he loved the taste of the melting chocolate on the tea.

So Dad ate a big feed of meat, veg and spuds at 12.30 every day, without fail, on the dot. After the dinner, Mam would put up two plain biscuits with a mug of strong tea. Dad took one disdainful look at the plain fare and said:

"Woman, will you take away them workhouse biscuits? "

He was never a man for the same old, same old. Dad sought out exotic characters from as far away as two miles out the road.

There was Dad's great friend Sonny Canavan, the bodhrán maker who had a glass eye. Sometimes Sonny took out the glass ball, placed the marbled eye on the bar counter, and he would say: "Keep an eye on Nora" to the eye. Nora was Sonny's wife.

Sonny had a talking dog. Banana V was his name. When the dog barked out "bow wow", Dad said it was "go now". This was the only way of getting us to go up to bed when we were small and Dad was telling us the bedtime stories about the Irish superhero Mick Mulally, who saved the Amazon rainforests by peeing all over the burning trees.

But I still can't watch Dad on TV. I get too sad. I know this is terrible, because he left such a legacy. I so wish I could watch all those clips from the 'Late Late' with his pal and ally, Gay Byrne. And I know too there are many of you who would love to have just a snippet of a lost loved one telling a story.

I took my mother's death very badly and only started to come around a bit in the last few months. So in a way I didn't have any room to think of Dad.

The 90th has him back again in my thoughts. I can see him now with those arms swinging, the right shoulder dipped to one side, as he walks at a fierce clip around his beloved bogs and woods near the town he loved so well.

Now I'm beginning to enjoy him again.

The two of them were there for me when I fecked up everything. He knew the pub was my game. And when I asked for advice about writing, he said: "Just write the feckin' thing." I still use the best advice ever given to a writer when I'm half-tormented trying to think up what

I'm going to write, and the clock is ticking on at 10 seconds in the minute for the deadline time.

I am so proud of Dad. He took on the world, with Mam not behind him or at his side but right there in front of him. Mam was the bouncer in our pub until she was 88 years of age.

Dad was the first to take up the cause of the kids who were looked down on by society because their mothers weren't married. He took on the Government over emigration. Dad took on the Church over sex, or more accurately, the lack of it. 'The Field' explained why we kill over land and the play saved lives. Our people saw themselves in his plays and they knew then why they were the way they were.

He even wrote funny about domestic violence and got away with it. The humour was his most powerful weapon.

There's a play called 'The Change in Mame Fadden', which never gets an airing now, and the theme is all about the female menopause. Dad was Ireland's first male feminist. But he was useless around the house. Mam was in the hospital one time and Dad boiled an egg in the electric kettle.

The Seanchaí Kerry Writers Museum organised a big 90th this weekend here in Listowel, but it's only now I'm able for it. I opted out. I was too sad thinking back. Thanks so much to David Browne, Cara Trant, Tom Fitz and Vincent Carmody.

I have made up my mind to enjoy Dad from now on. I have him ready in my head now on autodial. The 90th has triggered the recollection of so many happy days.

I love you Dad and I miss you so much even though I know you are still here. Happy birthday dear Dad, happy birthday to you.

2

Some Say Good Riddance To Bad Rubbish — But For Me Filling Up A Skip Retold The Story Of Our Lives

April 6, 2019

' **A** SKIP is therapeutic," said the man collecting the big container from outside the back of our pub. The skip was full of piled-high rubbish which was in a way a bit like a layered dig on an ancient archaeological site.

The Vikings left combs, coins and shells. Ours was broken beer garden furniture, cracked toilet cisterns, damp duvets, treacle paint buckets and old clothes left by the inebriated and not so much as stylish enough for the togging out of a scarecrow.

The remains of the torn, the broken and the useless were piled high. I didn't dump anything of importance. There is no doubt but that we often buy so much we want but don't need.

Goodbye then to the tailor's mannequin I used to scare off would-be robbers. One woman was sure there was a body dumped in the skip when she saw a leg sticking out.

This was the story of a home and a pub, a family, of all of our lives and the memories came back incrementally with the finding of every piece of home lore. One memory triggered another. Forgotten history was brought back before our very eyes.

There was the treasury of old photographs. My Mam was kissing Uncle Dan goodbye at Kennedy. That one made me cry. It was the last time they met.

Then there was one of Mam and Dad with their arms around each other and you could see how much they loved each other. They are still together... somewhere. The photo was a reassurance they are still very much in love... wherever.

We found a whole story of old Christmases and me there with my big mad head of black curls whooping it up with the brothers. There were letters from Dad to my sister Joanna. He wrote of how much he missed her when she was away in college and how he was so happy to have finished writing his novel 'The Bodhrán Makers'.

We found Joanna's old record collection and my Greek grammar. I was in the last class in Ireland to study Greek and I loved it. I gave an hour going back over the phrases from far away and long ago.

We found my granddad's collection of Charles Dickens and a letter from Brendan Kennelly to me, praising a book I wrote when I was badly lacking in confidence after a terrible review.

It wasn't just the going back but the learning of life lessons. I resolved to write to people who I admired and to praise them.

The skip man was right. This going back was good for me. I couldn't even get myself to watch Dad on YouTube because it made me too lonesome.

I spent days going through the big plastic bags stored in the attic in the extension our parents built when we were teenagers. It was a gentler way of reminiscing as I slowly and carefully sifted through the story of us.

There was an old football jersey I permanently

removed from the Listowel Emmets kit bag by way of a secret protest. It had 17 on the back and I was peeved I didn't make the first 15. I came across a picture of our under-14 football team. We won a lot together and we lost a lot together but we always stuck together.

I had it in my head to bring it to Maurice Walsh, my pal since babies' class. He passed away on Thursday. I loved that man. He always had my back, on and off the pitch. Maurice backed me even when I was wrong. He was a fine footballer, brave and honest. The old photo is in front of me now.

I found buried treasure there among the dust and the cobwebs. There was a clearing too. I could see the contour of the rooms in our tiny upstairs over the pub and out the back where us boys were moved. The decluttering was like setting a bird free from a cage.

Soon enough the skip went public. The skip foragers were looking for items that may have been of interest to them but of little use to anyone else. One woman took a green-from-the-mould plastic chair with a broken bottom that was a cracked buttock pincer.

Then late at night I spotted a man bringing two bags of assorted rubbish, a child's car seat and a fur coat made from what looked like rat hide.

I left him be.

All he had to do was ask and I would have said "belt away" but I'd say getting permission was no good to him. It was like raiding an orchard when we were kids. The people who owned the orchard would have given us the apples no bother but there was no fun in that.

Then this lad wearing a waist-coat asked how long we were going to keep the skip outside the back door. "It's an eyesore," he said, "and will draw vermin." He wasn't even from Listowel — the tidiest town in Ireland.

"The skip is here for good," I said to him. "We got a grant from the Arts Council. The skip is an installation."

Off he went, full of fight, looking for some victim to unload his angst upon over the shameful carry-on by the Government.

I was going through the last bag when I found the lost one-act play. It was called 'Mother Columba' and was written by Dad in the early Sixties. The play was written in his own hand, in pencil, in tiny writing, barely readable. The play was never heard of and it was about life in a convent.

I think Dad may have chosen not to go on any further as Auntie Kathleen was a young nun at the time and he was afraid he might embarrass her.

The skip man was right. There was therapy there upstairs as I sifted through lives and times in the cold air. I probably wouldn't have been able to face the looking back if it didn't happen upon me accidentally in the course of the tidying.

The skip man's name is Anthony Sexton from Templeglantine in west Limerick. Anthony told me of how his customers told him the filling of the skip was like watching a documentary of the story of their lives.

We meet philosophers in all sorts of places and situations.

There was a sense too of just how much we lived. The findings were a timeline through a life I had lived but largely forgotten.

I felt I had lived longer than I thought I had. Looking back without tangible and tactile reference points can be too condensed, too quick.

There is no time to think and no hints. The skip doesn't skip.

3

Gavin's Greats Play Glory Game But Kingdom On Rise

September 16, 2019

Today the skies are blue and the people of Dublin sing I love you.

We in Kerry salute you Dublin. You are the first county to win the fabled five-in-a-row. Dublin, you have won the most important All-Ireland ever played.

Jim Gavin's team can win every way. Dublin mix art and pragmatism. The champions have not only given football a makeover, they have made the beautiful game beautiful again.

And as we have written here before, they are changing Dublin for the better.

When small boys and small girls wear the mantle of blue, the children are bestowed with the gift of togetherness, the freedom of the city and the keys of the county.

Jason Sherlock gave every child the right to play for Dublin when he became Dublin's darling. It was fitting then that Jayo became one of Jim Gavin's managers.

In time the historians may well deem the gift of inclusion as the greatest achievement of this team.

For this reason the GAA must never partition Dublin. And for this reason, the funding for the children of Dublin must never be cut.

I am hurting today. Kerry were always the makers and the takers. We were the ones who wrote every other county's horrible history

There is no doubt but that Dublin were the better team on Saturday. We can't blame the referee, which is a great relief.

Conor Lane was fair. He was never swayed by the roars of the crowd and while Kerry may complain about the Camino of steps for the goal, it can be said the referee was not the reason we lost.

Kerry were beaten by a team who played some of the finest football of the five years, and indeed some of the finest football ever seen.

Kerry, you gave your all and we can ask no more. The way we were is the way we are. Kerry were true to our tradition. We did not play to contain or curtail. It was real football. We had a cut, a right cut, and made sure Dublin earned the right to win the five. And in the drawn game, we gave Dublin the fright of their lives.

Our team are heartbroken. But they must stick with it. The heartbreak will be cured by the winning of an All-Ireland. Our progress this season has been spectacular.

We now have two All-Ireland finals in our memory stick. Dublin were bigger, stronger and fitter. The worry was the drawn game would have taken too much out of Kerry and the replay was played at a savage pace with non-stop off-the-ball movement by the champions. It would be easier to track Whitey Bulger.

It takes two or three years to get to Dublin's level of fitness. Kerry must look at bringing in the top people in the world, whatever the cost may be.

Kerry will beat Dublin. It's not a never, it's a when.

So to our heroes I would say the resistance starts

today. The vital signs are strong. Our midfield broke even, at the very least. The Kerry defence had a growth spurt over the last two weeks. Our attack opened up Dublin several times over.

Let there be no blood-letting then back home. The players should take no notice of the sheep worriers who roam the net at night.

Men, your own people love you like sons and brothers.

Peter Keane and his management team have brought on this team so much in such a short space of time. They too are on a learning curve. Peter is honest and intelligent.

In Tim Murphy, we have an excellent chairman. He is solid, sound and dependable. We are as good as Dublin at football. That's a good place to start from.

Today though is Dublin's day ,and rightly so.

You would wonder what will happen if Jim Gavin and Stephen Cluxton retire. Will the next Dublin movie be called The Return of the Startled Earwig? The Dublin manager says the team is player-led. Dublin are Jim-led. He has done Dublin some service

On Friday night, I had a quiet chat in our back yard with Bernard Brogan, the elder. He stole the best-looking girl on our street.

I whispered, "It won't be as bad if young Bernard wins five in a row." There would have been no five but for the Brogan boys - Alan and Bernard junior won the middle years for Dublin.

There are many more too who must be praised. Perhaps the most important is Pat Gilroy who was the manager in the breakthrough year of 2011. He banished the monkey who lived for so many years on Dublin's back to the Phoenix Park.

There's a kind of funereal hush here in our town on this grey sky morning.

But we weren't reared to lie down and die, were we? We were bred to be brave.

We were brought up to fight to the end, and not the bitter one either, but the end when Kerry win.

Kerry have often been beaten, but we were never broken.

4

Inspiring Time In The Company
Of American Dreamers

March 19, 2016

WHEN I stepped into the White House, I felt as if I was walking in someone else's shoes. I was there representing my family in the United States. Friends too and all of us who truly believe in the American Dream.

My auntie Anne and my uncle Teddy emigrated when they were teenagers. Teddy and Anne have been in America for over 60 years now. Anne is on my dad's side and Teddy is on my mother's side. Because of health issues they are unable to come home on holidays. They miss Ireland so much and we miss them.

Anne and Teddy used to love coming home.

So there I was representing Teddy and Anne and all of the cousins we have in The States from Kentucky to San Francisco. From New York to Florida. They came over here to America when there was nothing for them at home.

My daughter Laura won the family draw for the plus one and as we walked in through the doors of the White House for the President's St Patrick's Day party, we heard the lifting, lilting pipe music as were going through security and it stirred the heart.

We walked in as if we were in Croke Park following on

behind the Artane Band. Immensely proud, in our best clothes, and all those Irish-American family and friends marching alongside in my mind's eye.

President Barack Obama's speech and the whole emotion of the occasion has changed my view of Irishness, of what it means to be one of us. Our greatest challenge as a nation is coming at us fast and hardly anyone here has a plan. The world is moving house and most are heading for Europe.

We wandered around the White House as if it was our very own. There we met three Prime Ministers. One of the negotiators of the peace process told us it was here in Washington away from the glare of cameras and reporters that the Peace Process was brokered.

"Bitter enemies became firm friends. President Clinton played the sax and sang his heart out until four o'clock in the morning. And the other side didn't seem so bad after all." Just being there inspires us. The constant complaining here in this country would wear you down but the Americans really are a can-do people. 'Is féidir linn' should be our morning and evening prayer.

We were invited by Kevin O'Malley, the American ambassador to Ireland. I met him in Listowel just a few days after the Berkeley tragedy. He is a quietly spoken man whose parents were Irish. You could see how emotionally involved he was.

Ambassador O'Malley cares. There were direct calls to the White House and our boys and girls were brought home to their grieving parents within a few days of the accident.

Ambassador O'Malley is in Ireland to represent the interests of the United States but he continually supports the bringing of jobs to our country. And much more. The Ambassador is as much an Irishman as an

American. He understands better than most what is to be an Irish American. His parents came from our west and now their son is the American ambassador to Ireland.

We were told to go right up the rope to get the chance to shake hands with the President.

There's this bunch who go every year from Moneygall and by now they have become Washington insiders. Henry Healy, the president's cousin, is Mr Washington.

Ollie Hayes, the president's favourite publican and his good buddy, was there too as was Fr Joe Kennedy, the amiable PP of Moneygall and another cousin young Billy. Henry and Billy had Twitter and Facebook hopping. They really are smart and do all they can to boost Moneygall, which is as it should be.

And so we bring the first exclusive. While the rest of us were outside the rope looking in at the President and the Vice-President, the Moneygall boys were hanging out with their buddy Barack.

He told the boys he was dying to get back to Ireland and there were a few golf courses he wanted to try out. He has a genuine affection for his Moneygall friends. Last year he was heartbroken when he had to refuse the lads' invitation to "come on out for a few quiet few pints".

So Ollie and myself were there, two country publicans, drinking green champagne in the drawing room of the White Hose and he telling me without any sort of affectation all about his chat with his buddy Barack.

President Obama's speech was truly inspiring. He really does feel Irish and the opening line of "I'm here to welcome my own people" brought the house down.

He spoke scathingly of the racist bigot Trump who just the other day called Mexican emigrants rapists and promised to build a wall around Mexico. Don't vote for him. He'll be after the Irish next.

The President's message was we should be knocking walls, not putting them up. The words were meant not just for Trump but for all of us and especially our friends up north.

President Obama spoke of the Irish blood running through his daughter's veins. And when he mentioned the Moneygall boys, I let a big roar our out of me. The roar put the President off his stride.

So he looked over to me and asked, "Are they here?" And I said, "Yes, right at the back of the hall." So you ask me do I know Barack? We had a chat didn't we? In the White House. And then the President went on to say he was still trying to have the Irish undocumented made legal. He meant every word. There was fire in his eyes and fire in his voice.

Enda Kenny is at his best in America. His speech was truly inspirational and he quoted a line we wrote just after the election as he walked with the President. "Service is forgotten when sins are forgiven."

Laura got to shake the President's hand he gave her a big smile. I was knocked over by a big lady who ate for both countries. It was like being hit by Ultan Dillane from Tralee.

So how have I changed? Until the White House I felt we needed to limit numbers of the oppressed who were coming in to our country.

Well, I now believe Ireland has to do all we can to bring in the less fortunate and make an Irish Dream. We can do so much good. The GAA can do so much good.

And so too can all of our sporting organisations. Sport binds and sporting heroes break bigots.

Addis, the taxi man from Ethiopia, was driving us

to the White House. When were outside the East Wing he said, "You know my friends some day my son can be President of America". So how about the Irish Dream?

We must redefine Irishness to include all of the boys and girls who have come here for our support, our love and their chance of a better life.

And maybe the day is not far away when a young African-Irish boy will take the Sam from the president of the GAA and really live the Irish Dream.

I was shocked to hear the bloomers are no longer available. These were the best contraceptives of all and were approved of by the Church which was down on sex, unless one of themselves was having it.

5

Every Man In The Country Should Be Made To Dress Up As A Woman For Five Nights — If Only To Give It Up

January 5, 2019

THIS is what was said to me by the woman in the underwear department of the big store when I asked to buy a bra and knickers, for myself.

The ever so polite salesperson didn't seem in the least bit fazed. "You'd be amazed," she said, "who asks me for what's in here."

Sure isn't the country full of transvestites and cross-dressers. Fair play to them too. To each, his and her own.

To be more specific I was looking for black tights, pink bloomers and a large bra for the fuller figure.

I was shocked to hear the bloomers are no longer available. These were the best contraceptives of all and were approved of by the Church which was down on sex, unless one of themselves was having it. The bloomers were double-gusseted and elasticated below the knee, for purity. It would be easier to get through strands of barbed wire in World War I.

I went to a smaller store.

I settled for large white panties with long legs like football togs and plenty of room inside for the extremities women do not have to cope with. I had to go for the XXL and I didn't try them on.

The lady in the shop sized me up from bottom to toe. Her conclusion was "you're a small man, but you're a big woman".

There was no charge.

The sign on the counter read "underwear and bras cannot be returned under any circumstances". And who could argue with that? I needed to wear the knick-oomers five nights in a row so. The lady was spot on. The knick-oomers fitted perfectly and were as soft as eiderdown on the skin.

I couldn't find a bra to fit me. I never knew bras were measured all the way around. It seems the back is included in the calculations. The size that suited best wasn't in stock and was something like a 46A, as in the buses, or a 99, like as in the ice creams. Whatever it was I forget, but we are talking big numbers here.

I blew up two balloons. I couldn't see my feet, which was very dangerous, and when I went to the toilet I had to remove my boobs. It was like learning to walk all over again. I was banging off everyone. My special awareness had to be reconfigured. I was always very bad at the parking. A garda said to me one time: "You didn't park that car, you abandoned it". It was as if there was an exclusion zone all around me. People backed off.

The worst part was the tights. One of my toes had grown long and pointy. The tights were torn and a fireman's ladder climbed up all along the length of my leg.

The tights were borrowed by a friend from his wife without her permission. The brand was called Alo Yoga. We're talking a hundred here or maybe more. That's fifty a leg and one leg was only fit for the bin. If I waxed my legs, well then that cost more again.

I had my chest waxed for charity and the hair took

years to grow back, I had to wear a top on the beach in case lads thought I was trying out for a place in a boy band comeback tour.

Leggings went on inside the tights as my floral, elasticated, one-size-fits-all skirt was very light and only fit for summer picnics.

I had to go to the chiropodist to be shod or the new tights would be torn to pieces.

The make-up took an age to put on. There isn't a part of the face that goes untouched and several types of brushes are used to apply the paint but I did find that part very relaxing. You are made to feel special.

It's also a day's work going to the toilet. You have to be very careful all the undergarments do not get tangled up, or fall on the floor which may not be pristine. You wouldn't want to be in a hurry.

I had to go out to the car for my manuka honey as my throat was as if it was grated by a potato peeler and salved with sandpaper dipped in hydrochloric acid. But am I complaining? No, not at all. When a man says he has the flu, some, but definitely not all, of the women will automatically diagnose man flu.

The graveyards of Ireland are full of men who were afraid to say they were sick. I heard lately of an epitaph that read: 'I REALLY DID HAVE PNEUMONIA'.

As I was saying before I mentioned a man's right to be sick, I was on the way out to the car for the manuka when this lad wearing a woolly hat couldn't keep his beady eyes off my new breasts. He perved me. It must be tough on women, all the same.

So I say to him, "Hey boss, I'm a man."

"So what?" says he.

I didn't go out in public again until Wednesday last, the opening night of the panto 'Goody Two Shoes', which is brilliantly directed by Donal Whelan and is choreo-graphed by the genius of Jo Jordan, who brought Kate Winslet in to John B's for a drink and I hadn't a clue who she was.

As I was saying earlier up the page, it isn't easy being a woman. I was sweating up under the lights and all the clothes. The sickness would have done for an ordinary man but I soldiered on. The rest of the cast carried me.

I am terrible for remembering lines and I missed most of the rehearsals due to work commitments. So I made up my own lines.

Right in the middle of the panto I stopped the show for a commercial break. I told the audience knickers were down all week in the January sales.

The man in the woolly hat who perved me was only a few rows up from the front. He never took his eyes off me and he had this pervy smiley face on him all through. One of my co-stars said he might appear at the back stage door with a bunch of flowers.

Every man in the country should be made to dress up as a woman for five nights.

We still have a few tickets left for tonight and tomor-row night. The proceeds go to local charities.

And then I will ceremonially hand back the silk scarf, my shawl, the three pairs of torn tights, the gold high-heel toe-crippling shoes, my black leggings and the knick-oomers, which were very warm and very comfort-able, but that's me done with being a woman, forever.

6

Neighbour, Mentor, Friend: Why Johnny Cahill Personified All That Is Good About Life In Small Places

February 9, 2019

SOMETIMES when travellers describe small places, they say "blink and you'll miss it". They were never in Dunnamaggin and never met Johnny Cahill.

The daily deeds taking place in small places are the stories of our time, and of all time.

Johnny Cahill was a Kilkenny hero and he was laid to rest on Monday last, among his own in the old wooded cemetery 'neath Kilree Round Tower.

Johnny was 93. He had a good run.

Andy Hickey, Johnny's neighbour and friend, was only 39 when he passed away.

His wife Anne looked after their eight children and the family farm with all of her considerable might.

Anne kept on working through her loss. She had to. A farm never sleeps. Anne won her battle. Her sons took over and Anne has "25 and a bit grandchildren now".

Noel Hickey, Anne's son, won nine senior All-Ireland medals for Kilkenny. Maybe Noel was the greatest defender of all time. He is as tough and strong as any man from the hard work. Like his mom, he kept on going, no matter what.

Anne spoke of how Johnny mentored Noel when he took over the family farm. "Johnny sat up in the tractor with Noel when he was ploughing, and if he was a quarter of an inch out Johnny would pull him up on it. If there was something to be done, it would be done right.

"My son Jim took over milking the cows and Johnny helped him too. He was always talking to them, reminding them — have you done this, have you done that — advising, and always out for their good."

Tomorrow Johnny's beloved Dunnamaggin will play Castleblayney in the All-Ireland Junior Hurling final in Croke Park. Dunnamaggin have never won an All-Ireland club title.

Jim is now the GAA club chairman. Noel and his seven brothers and sisters were always told to back up their own place by Anne. They are very much rooted in the community.

Think of all you miss when you blink through small places. There is a context to life in such places that is simple in its own way, and the local pub is the hub of the small place story. And the other day my brother John, or Seán as they call him in Kilkenny, tracked down the man who fell out of the ambulance outside our pub.

It was 1977 and an ambulance was speeding along Market Street in Listowel when the back door of the vehicle swung open. The patient inside came flying out and off he went free-wheeling down the road.

The flying patient was strapped into the stretcher and he survived. We often spoke about the flying patient in our pub and recently the riddle of the man on the stretcher was solved. He was Seán Delaney from the village of Kells, which forms part of Dunnamaggin parish.

Seán claimed he got a dose of food poisoning, or some other gastric illness, and that the ejection out the back of the ambulance saved his life because it also dislodged everything he ate.

Seán was reloaded and a few minutes later he declared himself fit to go back in to the Listowel Races. He has made a full recovery.

The Delaney pub has been in the family for seven generations and Seán will be in Croke Park tomorrow, as will every man woman and child in Kells, Dunnamaggin and Kilmoganny, the three villages that make up the parish.

I wonder if Seán serves the new cocktail. It's called the Shane Ross, with one part orange and one part lemon.

The farming, the hurling, the neighbourliness, the post office and the pub are under threat as never before. Too many of us are blinking through.

Poor Johnny couldn't go to the pub in his later years as he was afraid of getting caught for being over the limit, even though the old man only ever had the few pints.

But there was a big party in his house every Christmas morning, for the men, while the women cooked the dinner. It was all hurling and farming, and a bit like a men's shed. Then the phone would ring and the neighbours would head for their own homes.

Anne laughs at the thought of all the men listening to Johnny on Christmas morning.

"He had the house and farmyard so neat and so tidy. He left nothing go to waste. I saw him in our yard scraping up the last little pieces of grain for Noel during the harvest. He gave my family a great education."

Anne called to see Johnny in the home before the semi-final against Cloughduv of Cork, back just a few weeks ago. "I thought he was turning the page. Johnny was dying several times but then you would see him at the match. Two days later, he was at the semi-final on the side-line down in Dungarvan. He got his niece to bring him. The lads were saying it was such a pity he couldn't make the final but then someone said "if we win he will surely be mentioned in Croke Park. Johnny would love that".

Good luck to Castleblayney whose achievement in reaching the final is truly a well-earned sporting miracle of our times.

We chatted about the loss of Andy in 1983 and Anne says "you have me going now", but she gathers herself, as she had to do, I'm sure, so many times over the years.

"Johnny was like a grandfather to my family. He travelled the country following the lads at the hurling. Visitors would come to see Noel from all over and then in would come Johnny and he would say 'ye better be going now' and the two would talk farming and hurling. Johnny kept it simple and lived a simple life."

Noel is still playing at 38. Now for the first time in his career, he will play a big game tomorrow without Johnny to advise and cheer him on.

When Johnny's coffin left St Leonard's church last Monday morning, his club gave him a guard of honour.

Noel Hickey, the holder of nine All-Ireland winner's medals, lovingly placed his four-in-a-row All-Ireland winning jersey on the coffin of his adviser.

Farming life goes on 365 days a year, come what may. There is no day off. It was back to work for Noel.

Noel's wife Elaine came in to see her mother-in-law. She told her about Noel.

Elaine said: "Noel is up on the tractor all morning long, keeping the yard clean and tidy."

7

Allowing Gay People In Ireland To Marry Is A Basic Human Right...
July 3, 2012

H E was an old man. How old I couldn't tell you. To the very young, the old are older than the Ice Age. We were afraid of him though. Wondered how fast he could run. Was that snail-slow, flat-feet walk without backswing a ruse to lure us young lads into his deadly embrace?

Joe wasn't his real name but that's what we'll call him.

We were scared of Joe but there was the thrill of being chased, which we saw as no more than another street game like 'hits' or football.

The young lads would call out "queer" and then run away as fast as they could in case old, slow Joe would grow wings. Joe worked in the town and wasn't married. He lived in a tiny flat over a shop.

The man was never charged with anything but, as a small boy, I believed in the primacy of rumours. Possibly the poor man was gay. A man who knew about such things told me so.

It was Ireland in the late 1960s and it happened in Everytown. The taunting, the sniggers behind pointing fingers and the crude jokes.

We can only guess at how many gay men and women

lived an underground lie of a life. Their sexuality stifled and sullied by the treacherous old cabal of church and State.

Homosexuality was a crime and a sin. The same church that ran an in-house travel agency for parish-less paedophiles, condemned homosexuals as perverted outcasts.

For those living a secret life it must have been something like the Jews hiding out for fear of the Nazis.

There was a gradual liberalisation of Irish society in the 1970s. I was in the company of a gay pal in a pub one night when an ignorant man asked my drinking companion if he was gay, only he didn't use that word. The expression I think was "are you a pillow biter, so?"

I cringed for my friend. We all knew he was as gay as Christmas and none of us gave a damn.

The pub stopped talking, in the same way as when a low-type gunslinger enters a Wild West saloon and the piano player hides under his chair.

Our friend's reply was the first time I ever heard a gay Irishman admit his sexuality.

"I just help out when they're busy," he said. The pub erupted in a spontaneous outburst of supportive laughter.

Back then we all watched a show called 'Are you Being Served' starring a very camp actor who had the funny walk and the swan-a-drinking bent hand gesture. His catchphrase was: 'I'm free'.

Gay people walked funny and talked funny on TV.

The stereotyping was the cause of one poor lad I knew 'having the gay-ness bate out of him' by his brothers.

There was the 'gay walk game'. You pretended there was a coin between the cheeks of your bum and the winner was the hero who kept the imaginary 50c in situ the longest. I don't think this was homophobic because we weren't, it was just messing ... but there must have been closeted gay people watching and how tough that must have been for them.

That was then, and now the State has broken from the unholy alliance. It took until 1988 and even then it was Europe that forced us to decriminalise homosexuality in the Norris Case ... but the church and the infallible Pope are steadfast in their beliefs.

Yes indeed homosexuality is still a sin in the eyes of the church. Note that's the church. Jesus, I would like to think, wouldn't be as harsh on men and women who are different just because the roulette balls in the hormone game wheeled into different chambers.

I had the great good luck to be in the company of the kindly Ryan Tubridy on the morning of the first civil ceremony. The civil ceremony is almost a gay marriage. I was waiting to be interviewed. The two lads were chirping away to Ryan and then without warning he asked me if I would like to wish them well.

What was I going to say 'sorry for your troubles' or 'you walk up to the altar owning 100 acres and come down with only 50?'

Of course, I wished them all the best and, as I did, it dawned on me they wouldn't be allowed up to the altar and, strictly speaking, they weren't married either in the eyes of the church or State. I thought of Joe and thousands like him.

And the couple for all their love, fussing and excitement weren't really getting married. The distinction is only straight people of the opposite sex can get married in Ireland.

The Dublin Pride week is just over and gay-ness was celebrated in all its diversity but there must come a time when there will be no need to highlight gender differences.

Some of these gay events bring us back to the funny-walk days. We tend to concentrate on the outrageous, the flamboyant and even the exhibitionist. The ordinary gay men and women can be genuinely embarrassed by this. It's not that they want to hide their sexuality. It's more a question of, as one man told me: 'I'm gay, so what'.

The ban on gay marriage is a form of institutionalised apartheid.

On Sunday, the Tánaiste said he would support a referendum which would legalise gay marriage.

Gay people should be allowed to say the words 'we're married'. It's no more than a basic human right.

We owe that much at least to Joe and all the Joes.

8

You'd Want To Be A Right Lúbán Not To Enjoy The English Language As It's Spoken In All Corners Of Our Island

February 23, 2019

WE speak a number of different versions of the English language in this country. Our linguistic log started in Cork city. We travelled from there to west Limerick and ended in John B's, when Derry came to Kerry.

I was walking along the quays of Cork this week when I noticed a window full of second-hand books. The window was almost like an extra room for the small shop and the books were arranged in tiered rows like the stands in a football ground.

The books on the bottom tiers had to be retrieved by means of a callipers on the end of a pole, of the type used by litter pickers to save their backs. The polite and patient shopkeeper climbed up on a stool inside the shop. She manoeuvred the pincer dexterously and retrieved the book.

Just then this older man came in to the bookshop. He gave the name of his book in his fine, real and traditional Cork accent.

"Please Miss," he said, ever so politely, "can you get me "Maaaawrdur is Easy."

The bookseller was originally from somewhere in Eastern Europe. Her English was flawless, better than mine, but I'm sure she never heard the word maaaawrdur before.

The name of the book had to be repeated several times over but the erudite bookseller still couldn't find the book 'Maaaawrdur is Easy'.

I knew what maaaawrdur meant. I spent three of the happiest years studying in UCC.

I am back in Cork once a week to do a slot on 'The Today Show' on RTÉ One, which is aired on Friday afternoons and repeated over the weekend. Work was never such fun and I have fallen in love with Cork city all over again. I knew well what maaaaawrdurr meant but I was enjoying the listening in so much, I kept my knowledge to myself.

I'm sure I must have told you the story of the wasp here before but it's a long time since I did. Revision is essential maintenance.

Cork has its own word for wasp. The word is wazzie.

The little boy is out playing in the garden, and he gets stung.

"Mammy, mammy," cries the little boy, "I'm after being stung be something."

Mammy replies, "Woz 'e a wazzie, woz 'e?"

I made great friends with the Cork lads in UCC. The expression of encouragement "doubt ya boy" meaning 'I wouldn't doubt you' was used a lot in the UCC football team when I was playing. My alma mater won the Sigerson Cup this week. Billy Morgan and Dr Con Murphy mentored us back when I was playing and these famous football men guided UCC to another big win.

One of the lads might come out of a particularly tough exam and he would say, "That was maaaawrdur, Keano." Yes, I was Keano as a boy, even before Roy.

I did eventually intervene in the book shop on the quay, and I hope the old boy enjoyed 'Murder is Easy' by Agatha Christie.

I hope there is never a homogenisation of Cork speak. Abbeyfeale in west Limerick is only a bridge away from north Kerry. We speak much the same language. But the west Limerick dialect has more of the Irish in it. More than half of the population of west Limerick spoke Irish in the 1850s.

Séamus Ó Coileáin from Athea lectures in NUIG and he came up with many examples of the infusions and seasonings at a lecture to celebrate the Tionol festival in the town. Thanks to Dónal Ó Murchú of the best trad band Four Men and a Dog for sending on the list.

Glaise is a stream. A tricky corner forward would make a lúbán out of his opponent.

Ráiméis "is the name we give to a wrong account of anything" or nonsense. Balbh is when someone has a speech problem, as in "he was balbh with the drink".

I use these words all the time without ever thinking where they came from. It seemed to me everyone knew what it was I was talking about but that's not the case. Pusheen is kitten and banbh is a piglet in our speak.

Everyone around here knows the meaning of the words but people from outside the confines of north Kerry and west Limerick weren't sure of the meaning.

I spoke to a young woman the other day who described the man who broke the wing mirror of her car as a bit of a mee-aah, which comes from the Irish word mí-ádh.

The richness is kept on by the younger crowd and isn't it very handy to own your own words when you don't want people to know what you are talking about? Talking funny can be fun too.

And we had some fun on Sunday night last when the Derry twins and one of their husbands visited our pub.

The Derry girls were 60-year-old twins who didn't look 60 between them and they were wild good looking. Wild is used a lot in their part of the world instead of the very boring 'very'.

The Derry girls hailed from Seamus Heaney country. There was a cadence and a nuance in their every word, which was as much Scottish in terms of intonation and flavouring as it was Irish. There were lots of yons, wees and wilds.

It's no wonder Heaney had the ear for the poetry. Alice and Marie had us crying with the laughter. Martin was the prompter. They referred to each other as "our Martin", or "our Marie", or "our Alice", as if they were all the one, and they were.

The Derry girls went to a removal some time ago. The twins had a quick peep in to the coffin, "to take stock of the corpse".

I interrupted the Derry girls before they rightly got going, in case I forgot to tell my story later on.

I told our new friends about the time I was sorrying for your troubles here at home. The deceased was laid out in the coffin beside us.

My co-mourner had a good look at the dead man. He nearly fell into the coffin.

"Billy," he said, "he looks very bad."

"He's dead, Dinny," I replied.

The Derry deceased looked his very best. One twin said to the other, "Hi, he looks wild well. He looks just like himself."

And her sister replied, "Why? Who else would he look like?"

9

Between Rockall And A Hard Place: The Warmonger's Answer To The Scottish Fishmongers

June 15, 2019

THE Basques, the Celts, the Vikings, the Normans, the Spanish, the Scots, the French and the English have all invaded us.

It doesn't take a military genius to figure out which of the above would be easiest to take out. It's the Scots. They have an even worse record in big battles than we do. And right now the Scots are coming on strong.

Last year, the treacherous Scottish Rugby Football Union refused to vote for us to host the Rugby World Cup. Now the Scots have claimed part of Ireland as their very own. The Scots have laid claim to Rockall, which is too small even for one-off housing. The Scottish have threatened to arrest the fishermen from Greencastle if they fish off Rockall. This is an act of war.

Isn't it ironic then that the Scottish First Minister, Nicola Sturgeon, is named after a fish? Her predecessor as leader of the Scottish National Party was a man called Alex Salmond and he was all for making Scotland great again. The annexation of Rockall is a red herring to distract people from the embarrassing fact the Scots voted to stay on as part of Great Britain. This tactic is similar to the one used by Margaret Thatcher, who fought Argentina when she was going bad in the polls. The best practice for invading another country is to pick on a place with hardly any planes or ships or soldiers. Ireland is temporarily under-strength right now.

The Scots haven't picked a name yet for the invasion of Rockall. The Americans are very good at thinking up top war games handles such as Operation Desert Storm for the first Gulf War. My own favourite is Operation Urgent Fury, the title given to the invasion of Grenada by the United States in 1983.

Sources close to the Scots working at the front suggest the Scots might just go for Operation Kilt Kill. There is still time to sue for peace, as my cousin Fergal is still in Africa.

Simon Coveney, our Foreign Affairs Minister, has gone for a measured diplomatic approach.

But if Vladimir Putin was in charge of Ireland, there would be Tricolours flying high tonight over Edinburgh Castle. The umbrella tips would be dipped in polonium and the massed choirs of 'Scotland the Brave' would be stilled by 'A Nation Once Again' or 'Ireland's Call' if the DUP join us.

I say we declare war on Scotland.

I go further. Let's not lose the element of surprise by declaring war. The fisheries police would hardly phone a den of poachers to declare they were about to make a raid.

The Scots have it coming. They invaded us first.

Ulster was planted by Scots Presbyterians in the 17th century. The locals were kicked out of their farms. We hadn't a day's peace ever since. The EU will be only delighted. How can Britain leave if we invade them? The US will surely back us, although President Trump also owns a hotel and golf course in Scotland.

It seems that while the seas around Rockall are full

of fish, the real wealth could be underneath the surface of the ocean. Most of the wars in recent times have been fought over the control of gas and/or oil reserves. We are well within our rights.

We must stop the Scots and stop them now. And what's next for the Scots? Will they go after Rathlin Island or even the Aran Islands? There's nowhere safe. The 'domino theory' caused the Vietnam War. It went something along the lines that when one country toppled over, the next one fell as well. Meanwhile, Ricky Noble's stag on Achill today goes on as planned.

The UN will go in to special conclave. We can use the excuse used by Hitler when he invaded the Sudetenland. Hitler's lie was that he was only annexing his neighbours to protect the Germans who were being blackguarded by the Czechs. President Putin maintained he was only invading the Ukraine to mind the people there who were of Russian descent.

Many of the ancestors of the Ulster dispossessed have settled in Scotland. There are more people of Co Donegal descent living in Scotland than in Co Donegal. Every Gallagher and O'Donnell in Scotland will rise up with us. All of Celtic will march with their own.

Celtic fans have been subjected to vile chants from the pro-invasion Glasgow Rangers fans over a good many years. There's our excuse, and now is the time.

The Army must be mobilised immediately. Only the Army mind. If we send gardaí the overtime would break the country.

We must move quickly while the parties of the left here at home are still trying to make up their minds whether we are imperialist warmongers fighting a war over oil or patriots reclaiming the lost rock of the Irish.

Our war is moral. Our struggle for freedom is legally justified.

History is on our side. Rockall is ours. The Wolfe Tones claimed Rockall many years ago. Now The Continuity Wolf Tones are ready to rouse the troops with the old refrain from 'Rock on Rockall', a big hit in the 1970s.

May the Seagulls rise and pluck your eyes/And the water crush your shell/ And the natural gas will burn your ass/And blow you all to hell...

I was just thinking there now, we might as well take the Isle of Man as we're at it. The British will probably just draw a line down the middle and give us half, just as they did with the Indian sub-continent and the Middle East.

The Irish have tried to stake a claim other than by singing for Rockall.

We must fight for those who went before us. A small Irish force, of one, invaded Rockall on July 8, 1975. Willie Dick bravely jumped from a ship named the Verve, captained by Michael d'Alton, a decorated veteran of D-Day.

I heard tell of a boy who was christened Michael Long, but one day his name was called out on the school roll as Long, Mickey. He was often slagged off after that like 'A Boy Named Sue'. I hope there will be no inappropriate remarks from the Scots over the name of our Rockall climber. Willie Dick patriotically scrambled up the slippery rock, measured Rockall, planted the Tricolour on the top and meticulously inscribed the record of the Irish invasion on a previously fixed British plaque. Ireland must follow on from Willie Dick and take what is rightfully ours.

PS: We can always give Scotland back afterwards if it proves too dear to run.

10

Heart-shaped Hole Solves Boot Puzzle

June 18, 2018

THIS is the story of four boots, several extraordinary women, Le Drop, and a panic attack.

Sister Eileen Keane, who gave of herself always, was laid to rest on Thursday last with her friends. Eileen taught in San Francisco for a good many years and then when she came home to Ireland the lovely lady from Ballylongford in North Kerry helped mind her grandnephew Jonathan Sexton every time his mother Clare became pregnant.

Jonathan wore a black armband for Eileen on Saturday when Ireland beat Australia. He was mad about Eileen who I think maybe she found what it was like to be a mom when she minded the Sexton kids.

The few Sisters of the Infant Jesus who are still left in our world sang a poignant rendition of 'Hail Holy Queen', which was audible barely above the birdsong in the still of the tiny burial plot of Drishane.

I was given Jonathan Sexton's boots by his family after the hymn was sung.

These were the boots he wore all through the Grand Slam. These were the Le Drop boots. Jonathan scored the winner against France with the last kick of the game from a place so far away from the French goal a nation had the time to slowly suspend time as we charted the progress of the boot to glory.

When I opened the boot bag, I knew I was in trouble.

There were four boots in the bag. Laura Sexton, Jonathan's wife, is seven months pregnant and she is up to her eyes minding two small kids. Laura is the rock. She had no problem with handing over the family heirloom. Laura didn't know which boot scored the Le Drop.

So what do I do? There is a bid in of ten grand on the boots. The bid was made by a Dublin GAA mom who paid the money up front but with the proviso that if the bid was bettered then the Anna Browne Fund could keep the money anyway.

The Dublin Mom stayed anonymous. She came into some money and was moved by the story of Anna who needs an operation to help her walk and take away the terrible pain she goes through every day and especially at night.

Anna's mother Evelyn has been campaigning night and day to raise the €100,000 needed to fund her daughter's operation in America. Before the story of the boots came out, Anna's fund was at €18,000. Now there's €84,000 in the bank. Evelyn booked the operation for August 14 next, even though she is well short of the target.

Evelyn cries a lot for her daughter, the worry of it all and the thought of raising so much money. The day Sister Eileen was laid to rest was the first anniversary of seven-year-old Anna's diagnosis of severe cerebral palsy.

I felt overwhelmed. I was the one who persuaded Evelyn to book the operation. But now we didn't even know the right boot to sell. The four boots were identical and it was impossible to distinguish one from the other. All we knew was Le Drop was kicked by a right boot, but which one?

Jonathan is in Oz and I got it into my head all was lost, and he wouldn't know either. I stopped on a bridge over the Blackwater and I was tempted to throw in one pair of adidas boots. Any time I ever got into trouble, it was because of a mad impulse to keep on digging. Only I would ever know about the drowned boots. But I didn't — couldn't do that to the Dublin Mom.

Now I know how Prince Charming felt when he was looking for that cracked young one Cinderella.

Our auctioneer Philip Sheppard advised that "the punters need certainty if they are to fork out big money for a piece of Irish sporting history, that might only come up once in a lifetime." Philip gave his services free of charge. He too is an Anna fan.

"Billy," he said, "there's a season for these auction sales, and it's not back on until September." Which of course is too late for little Anna .

I called the Dublin GAA Mom. If the Dub mom pulled out, the operation would have to be postponed. Out came the story. "Slow down," she said. "You what? Two?" The Dublin GAA Mom laughed for fully three minutes. "That's a great story," she said.

"Do you want your money back?"

"No, I do not? This is about the child, not the boots."

And I have never met his woman. I don't even know her real name.

I nearly hoped then, for a very short time, her beloved Dubs would go on to win the four-in-a-row.

Ireland won and I texted Jonathan. At 1.35am on Sunday morning, there was a text back from JS: "It's the one with a heart-shaped hole on the right boot, around where my big toe was. They were the Grand Slam, H Cup, league boots." Jonathan has never lost in these old raggedy boots.

I should have known. He gives such attention to detail and these boots are part of him, a very smelly part of him. There's a lesson there for those of us who panic. Most problems can be sorted out. It's funny now.

The people of Cork and Ireland have been so good. One pair of battered old boots for sale then, right now. And if there's anyone who can give even a single euro, you can do so on https://www.gofundme.com/annas-dream-to-dance .

Or send on a cheque if you can afford it, and if you can't well then a prayer for Anna will do just as much good.

11

Sexton's Smelly Old Boots Drop Another Triumphant Goal For Little Anna — And A Couple Of Rascals

December 1, 2018

JONATHAN SEXTON'S famous boots were sold off at €15,500 for the two. There was another 10 grand paid up front by way of bank draft by Betty Boots.

Betty's perfect 10 brought the total to €25,500 for the world's most famous (and smelliest) pieces of rugby memorabilia.

The auction at Sheppard's of Durrow wasn't at all what I expected it to be. I had this idea of a Lovejoy winking and nodding in his bids, at the back of a packed auction hall.

It's mostly all done online now but there was drama.

Betty Boots isn't the under-bidder's real name. Betty wishes to remain anonymous. She is one of the good people we seldom get to hear about.

Betty is a mom and a Dublin GAA fan who gave €10,000 to a small girl from near Mallow in Cork. She read here of the Browne family's battle to get their Anna to St Louis in the United States for a big operation.

Anna has cerebral palsy and the operation was a huge success. The bravest and bestest of small girls can run and walk to school now, but there are many more days of fight-back ahead.

There is little if any back-up provided in this country by way of aftercare. Anna is just back from Wales and a week of intense specialist physiotherapy. Her big sister Emma did every single exercise with Anna in St Louis and in Wales. Emma is the best sister ever.

A Cork man living abroad covered the cost of a full year's physio for Anna. He too wished to remain anonymous. The secret millionaire made a bit of money and he gets far more pleasure out of spending it than making it.

I got some buzz out of the auction in Sheppard's. There were six people taking online and telephone bids, sitting at a table in front of auctioneer Michael Sheppard.

Every time a bid came in, one of the bid-takers stood up and Michael called it out. It was all on screen and hundreds of people were watching live.

The bidding opened at €5 and moved on up as the bargain hunters gradually dropped out.

The bidding came to €1,000 and the next bid was €1,002. That was a worry but I knew we already had €10,000 in the bag from Betty. The auctioneers just wanted to acknowledge all the other bidders. The real action started when Betty's €10k was out-bid.

Betty was there. Only I knew who she was. She called in to John B's during the summer with her husband. He's a friend. Betty came in to some money — not a massive amount, mind, and she wanted to give something back.

Betty's money was spent, with her permission, on Anna's operation and she followed up with new bids of her own.

The bids from Ireland, Australia and the US were coming in fast and furious. Betty kept pace for a while and then she stopped. I will tell you why later on.

The final bid was €15,500. The boots were sold to an international businessman who is Irish. I have no idea who he is. Philip Sheppard, the MD of Sheppard's, told us the buyer planned to send the boots around to schools to encourage the kids to take up sport. The boots will stay in Ireland.

After the auction I met with an older lady outside Bowe's classy coffee shop, right next door to Sheppard's.

She opened up her purse. I couldn't help but look in. It was one of those small, old-fashioned purses from the days when people hadn't much. All I could see was a tenner, a five and some loose change. She took out the fiver but then she put it back in and gave me the tenner.

"That's for the little girl, for a Christmas box." What's your name, ma'am?" I asked. "Anonymous," she replied.

Durrow has reinvented itself from what seemed like the endgame when the town was by-passed by the Dublin-Cork motorway.

This is an old place with real people. Sheppard's employs 18 people and there are several spin-offs such as removers, upholsterers and furniture restorers. The auction was run very efficiently, with more than 1,200 lots sold off to bidders from all over the world.

I would urge city businesses to move to a place like Durrow. The houses are reasonably priced with good schools and even a 16km commute takes only 15 minutes.

We ate the best feed of beef ever in the Castle Arms and the lovely chips in the Copper Kettle takeaway are made from the finest of real spuds.

I met with Betty Boots after the auction and she explained why she stopped bidding. "I really wanted the boots but then I thought to myself, if I bid any more the family will lose out."

If Betty won, Anna would have benefited by another five thousand or so but if the Secret Millionaire won

THE VERY BEST OF BILLY KEANE

well then she would be up another €15,500. And so Betty Boots gave up on her dream.

When Jonathan heard the story he promised to send something nice on to Betty for Christmas.

There is someone up there looking after Anna.

I spoke to Jonathan a few weeks ago and asked him if we would beat the All Blacks. "Yes," was his reply. That was good enough for me. So we took the boots out of an earlier but bigger auction. The bet paid off.

On Sunday last, Jonathan was voted World Rugby Player of the Year. He is now officially the best player in the world.

It was the win over the All Blacks that swung it and increased the value of the boots that kicked the 48 metre 'Le Drop' to beat France in the last play in the Six Nations earlier this year. Yes, the boots were smelly. He wore the boots for every second of the Grand Slam, the European Champions Cup and the Pro14. Jonno never lost in those boots.

Evelyn Browne, Anna's mom, was wondering where the terrible smell was coming from when she went in to her sons' bedroom. She found Jonno's boots under the bed. Sean and James had "borrowed" the boots.

Evelyn fumigated the boots with every kind of anti-stink spray. I banned her from any cleaning of the boots after that. The smell was the smell of victory.

And so it was that two young hurlers playing for the Clyda Rovers under-16s and -17s came to be wearing a pair of football boots worth €25,500.

12

Jack's Army — I Became A Dad Instead Of A Lad And Missed The Bus

June 12, 2018

IT was in the summer of 1988 and Herself was slightly pregnant. The baby was due in July and the Euros were scheduled to start in June.

One of my more misogynistic acquaintances said it was all a cunning plot to keep me from heading off on the lash with the lads.

Later on when he was married himself, the same man was seen wearing an apron and there were stories he was baking scones with cinnamon.

The finals were held in Germany and I was offered a berth in an old minibus that had been decommissioned because the children were always late for school. The mechanic said we would be fine provided there were no hills on the way to the ferry in Rosslare, or in Brittany, or in the rest of France, or in Belgium, Holland and Germany.

The tour cartographer helpfully suggested Holland and Belgium were known as the Low Countries so there wouldn't be any hills and we would be in Stuttgart in loads of time for the England game.

The plan was I would travel over on the bus and come back by plane, just in case.

So I get to asking Herself seemingly innocent questions like "is there any danger the baby might decide to come out early?"

So, says Herself, "not if she's taking after you, seeing as you were never in time for anything in your life except matches".

There was no Googling anything back then. So I check up our set of leather-bound Encyclopaedia Britannica in Dad's study. The fountain of knowledge was stretched out the full length of a 2.5 metre shelf. The father would have some laugh if you told him back then there would come a time when you could put the whole lot in your pocket.

That was the problem about going away back then. When you were gone, you were gone. Mobiles cost a fortune and they were as big as ghetto blasters. Twitter, Skype and Facebook weren't yet invented and the phone system at home was up there, or down there, with the communication system on the Titanic.

So I became an amateur gynaecologist. The gist of my research was that a second baby is more likely to arrive early than the first. We were expecting the second instalment of Irish twins. Our first was born the September before and I would be away for ten days.

This was the summer I stopped being a lad and became a Dad. Conscience kicked in and I stayed put. Although truth to tell I regressed on many occasions since.

I waved the boys goodbye and they were full of their fun. Ireland in a big competition at last and me left at home. I consoled myself with the thought of the state they would be in when the crew returned home broke and broken.

Two weeks of eating more cheese burgers than Elvis, getting buckled from drinking beer out of German glasses as tall as Big Jack, falling out of bunk beds and getting drowned wet in army surplus flea tents.

The good news was I wouldn't get to meet Joxer. Christy Moore sang a song called 'Joxer goes to Stuttgart' four years after the '88 finals.

We all knew a Joxer. He was one of these Dubs the Dubs avoid, constantly going on about Bang-Bang, The Royal, and how his mother was knocked off the toilet when The Pillar was blown up, coddle, and the crack of his a**e forever showing because his pants were always at half-mast, and him not even a builder.

I knew there would never be a session like this again, ever. And I knew too we would be all on the one road. The fact was the Irish soccer fans really are the best. I did get to the Euros in France 28 years later and it was the greatest fun ever.

The team reared by Eoin Hand and managed by Jack Charlton played like the heroes they were. We were in a group with Russia, England and the Netherlands who beat us 1-0 with an 82nd-minute goal. The Dutch went on to win the competition outright.

There was a call from the lads on the house phone at three in the morning on the night we beat England 1-0.

Invitation

The singing in the background was 'Sean South' and, curiously enough, Abba's 'Waterloo'. I was put through to a German fraulein who told me she loved the Irish and it was very nice of me to invite her to stay with us for the summer. I issued no such invitation.

My pal was living with his mammy and he thought I would provide a safe house. I hung up and went back to mixing the Milupa for the night feed.

I was allowed out to the pub on furlough earlier that night. The place lifted when Ray Houghton headed the ball in to the English net. The ball, slow as a fly fisherman casting a line into a salmon run, seemed to take an age on the loop before it reached the back of the goal. It was the slowest goal ever. The pub went mad.

Dad, who was a fanatical GAA man, bought a drink for the house. Bachelor farmers who were seldom kissed were covered in lipstick. Men who fell out over ditch and dyke boundaries hugged. The cars beeped as if we were in Brazil, and mad young lads hung halfway out the windows like Cossack trick riders circumnavigating the circumference of a circus ring.

It was a starry, starry night. Home then and happy I was alive at such a time. I met up with my neighbour John Leahy and we walked together. John had it figured. He said this was the night we were rid of the post-colonial inferiority complex and Ireland was finally a nation once again, more than 60 years after independence.

I had a peep in at little Anne, fast asleep in her cot, and I thought there was nowhere else I'd rather be.

The phone rang again. "We're all part of Jackie's Army," travelled from an Irish bar in Stuttgart. The German girl offered to act as au pair. She had done a first-aid course and knew loads about delivering babies.

And the baby woke. I told Anne all about the great win we had that night over the English, and her sleepy lullaby was the night time nursery version of the old Mexican favourite 'Olé, Olé, Olé'.

13

Farewell To Uncle Teddy, The Emigrant Who Was Lonesome For His Home Place

November 21, 2016

THE call came through late on that Saturday night, just over a month ago. I was working in the bar. We were busy. The Brownes were singing and could be heard lilting over the chat like bird song above bee buzz.

Life is good, I was saying to myself. This is how pubs should be and I'm thinking the worst of the recession is lifting a little, at last.

The bar phone rang, the landline. We were in the middle of the busiest hour of the week. I left it a while. But the phone kept ringing. I answered. It was my cousin Conor.

"Bad news, Billy. Uncle Teddy passed away just a short time ago in Florida." I froze.

Then I went back to pulling pints, as if nothing happened.

On went the shop face.

It was like a sun shower when the tears came and the bar was closed. I was smiling and crying at the same time. Crying for the loss and smiling for happy thoughts of Uncle Teddy meeting up with his wife Joan, my mam, my uncles Jim and Dan, my Auntie Norrie and his parents.

Uncle Teddy was a year younger than my mother. She

passed away about a year ago. Mam was mad about him. In a way, I'm glad she went first. Uncle Teddy was her baby brother, her pet. My nana died in childbirth when Uncle Teddy was born and my mam mammied Uncle Teddy, small and all as she was.

My granddad died just a few years after Nana and Uncle Jim, who was the eldest, took over the farm. Auntie Norrie, who was a great people person, ran the shop for Jim. My mother served her time as a hairdresser in nearby Castleisland. Uncle Dan helped out until he left for America. They were a very united little family. There was no work at home back in the '50s and uncle Teddy followed Uncle Dan to New York.

The happy family was cut it two.

Teddy worked as a baggage handler in Kennedy. He married Auntie Joan and she was the kindest, most laid back woman who was ever born. Kids came along and they bought their first home.

All was going well until Uncle Teddy hit the bottle. He was a secret drinker. "The work was hard," uncle Teddy told me. There were late nights and early mornings. It was the tiredness that drove him to the drink. He would drink bottles left in the planes or sometimes he smuggled in his own to help him make it through the night.

The young emigrant was lonesome for his own place, his family here, and even though he never said it to me, I'm sure he was sad too for the mother he never knew.

Auntie Joan was a loyal Cork woman. She stood by him. Uncle Teddy's life changed forever and for the better on the day he joined Alcoholics Anonymous. My uncle found his faith again. Uncle Teddy was a devout Catholic and he was the oldest altar boy in Florida. He served Mass every day until he was 85.

My lovely uncle was conservative but he was

non-judgemental. Never once did he utter a cross word when his liberal nephew was writing cross words about the Church in this very paper.

He really did live the life of Christ, as best he could anyway. When I was at my very worst, through no one's fault but my very own, I remember telling him that I woke up one night in a drenched sweat. In the nightmare, I was at the bottom of a dark, damp well and I was trying to climb out. Uncle Teddy had the bottom of the well dreams too, he told me. "Everyone has their bad days and their bad dreams," he said. And I thought it was just me.

It was like an awake meditation when he spoke. His words were "time, time". And he was right. In time I did pull myself out of the well with the help of family and friends. I pass on his words to those who are battling with addiction in honour of my uncle.

"Time, time." I think he meant this too shall pass. Toughen a while and you will be fine.

Teddy was promoted and he moved to Florida. He was very happy there in Clearwater, near the ocean, and he did very well for himself. His kids loved him, his wife loved him and he loved them.

Auntie Joan died a few years back and Teddy still kept going to his AA meetings. But like so many emigrants, Uncle Teddy was more Irish than American. He came home every year.

My uncle was missing Auntie Joan and as we drove through the hill country near Rockchapel, where she came from, he would talk away about old times. There was the story about the man who asked for a pack of cigarettes on tick from the shop and came back from Australia 40 years later to pay his bill with the question: "Is there something there in the book I might owe ye for?"

Uncle Teddy always warned me to watch out for the drink and the tiredness behind the bar which sends many bar men reaching to the top-shelf for a quick pick-me-up.

My cousin James, who was a mental health professional for 40 years, has the gift of summing up people in one line. "Uncle Teddy had no anger in him", he said.

I think AA was a huge help and taught him how to let go. The aura of calmness spread to those around him and even travelled thousands of miles over the phone. Every summer, we host the "Uncle Teddies", as my mother called his friends. Most were Irish-American and the drinking gene travelled over the Atlantic. They ask for a diet coke. The "Uncle Teddies" are nearly all quiet people and a little bit shy. I often think shy people drink too much to get up enough courage to talk and make friends.

"We know your uncle Tim in Florida." Tim was his US name.

And after the second diet coke they open up. Uncle Teddy helped so many to give up the drink. It was the Christianity in him and he really did do his best to live the life of Christ. Deeds of love and grace are sometimes hidden in the repetition of the heroic anonymity of day-to-day living.

So there I was on Saturday night, all alone upstairs over the bar, in the sitting room, where my mam and Uncle Teddy spent hours talking about dad and Con Houlihan reciting poetry in their kitchen and bachelor farmers in their '70s proposing to Mam and Auntie Norrie, provided the dowry was big enough.

There I was crying those sun shower tears when I felt this serenity come over me. There, upstairs, from somewhere, I don't know where, came the thought that tonight Uncle Teddy would meet his mother for the first time in 86 years.

14

How Margaret The Giant Turkey Lived To See Another Christmas But Left A Trail Of Destruction Behind Her

December 22, 2018

MARGARET had a bounty on her head. She was dead meat they said. Her days were numbered anyway and the escape from captivity was considered to be no more than a stay of execution.

The animal rights activists compared her plight to that of the tiger in India. It seems tigers went about killing and eating natives and the locals were not happy about it. The story of Margaret's flight was world news and not just local. She was, after all, more than a metre tall and without doubt the biggest of her kind anywhere in the world.

The on-line news makers claimed Margaret was bigger than a wolf and every bit as ferocious; a killer, they maintained, and it was only a matter of time before she turned on humans.

People hereabouts, and even as far away as thereabouts, were terrified. Men who casually shoot wildlife began to congregate near the sight of the massacre of the sheep. Drones were put up as eyes in the sky. There was talk of closing the national park where Margaret was thought to be hiding out.

Margaret the so-called killer turkey was on the run. Christmas is open season for turkeys anyway but a so-called killer turkey has no chance of survival. (I use the term so-called deliberately because many of us thought Margaret was innocent, even though there were many who thought otherwise.)

Margaret was brought up free-range so she was used to foraging. But there were so many enemies such as foxes and stoats. The local sheep farmers formed a posse to hunt Margaret down.

And well you might ask, how could such a large turkey come to exist? It seems genetically modified feed found its way into the food chain.

Margaret's owner Mike Joe Mullaughatawny bought a cocktail of human growth hormone tablets, steroids, nandrolin, the pill and mixed the concoction into Noreen's grain-based breakfast. The egg laid by Noreen, Maureen's mother, was the size of an ostrich egg, which delighted Mike Joe no end.

Mike Joe had never won the Kerry Turkey Championship and he finished second on 37 occasions. His near neighbour Tom Big Bird won all 37 titles. Mike Joe was jealous and so he became a turkey cheat, but there was no dope testing.

Maureen won this year's competition hands down and the 'Guinness Book of Records' named Mike Joe's bird as the biggest turkey ever. The resultant publicity spread all over the world.

Mike Joe swore Maureen was fed only Kerry oats and new milk, or beastings. Then again, that's what all the drugs cheats say.

The trouble started when two lambs were ripped asunder by a vicious animal in the mountain at the back of Mike Joe's small holding.

Dogs would be the prime suspects in the normal course of events but some genius on a sheep forum claimed Margaret was suspect. The repeats, mis-informations, miscalculations and stupidities so often propagated in such fora turned conjecture into fact.

The sheep had been eaten but such was the frenzy on the sheep forum no one seemed to notice turkeys are not that partial to mutton.

The Sheep Farmers Association called to Mike Joe and asked him to have Margaret destroyed. Mike Joe had grown fond of Margaret but he was afraid of being sued even though she had never left the pen.

Mike Joe was always out for what was best for Mike Joe. He was going to sell Margaret to a big hotel and the plan was to bring her into the dining room, trussed, stuffed and roasted. There would be bugle music and a drum roll for the serving up of the world's largest ever turkey But no one would eat a sheep killer. The hotels would not buy Margaret. She was unsaleable.

For a time Mike Joe thought he might use Margaret as a guard turkey, like a German shepherd, which is a dog and not a person. Margaret was a quiet bird and though she had Mike Joe "ate out of house and home", she was a vegetarian.

The bills were mounting and Mike Joe decided to donate Margaret to the zoo. There she would be caged up beside lions and tigers but at least Margaret would be safe and — more importantly for Mike Joe — the zoo would have to feed her. The champion turkey owner had visions of a sign that read: 'MARGARET THE KILLER TURKEY', Breeder Mike Joe Mullaughatawny.

The zoo felt Margaret might not fit in too well with the pets in Pet's Corner, on health and safety grounds, and passed on Mike Joe's request to the Istanbul Zoo in

THE VERY BEST OF BILLY KEANE

Turkey. The Turkish zoo was very interested and sent over the head of the turkey enclosure to measure up Margaret. The sum of €25,000 was agreed, which made Margaret the most expensive turkey ever bought or sold.

The story might have had a happy ending for all concerned if it hadn't been for the puma.

There were sightings of a puma some time ago in Cork and when an animal resembling a puma was seen crossing the mountains between Cork and Kerry the panic started. The very same posse that was formed to shoot Margaret went out looking for the puma.

One of their number was of the opinion the killer puma was the assassin that murdered and ate the sheep. He expressed this theory and, as is often the case, theory became fact by repetition and endorsement by the opinionated who were not necessarily expert in turkey husbandry.

The puma, it seems, fled from the custody of an animal lover who smuggled him into Ireland illegally. The puma escaped when the owner accidentally opened the boot by pressing on the switch, while searching for his sunglasses in the glove box. The puma slipped away and was shot to pieces by the turkey posse a few miles on this side of the town.

The puma was found guilty by the lynch mob, the Turkish Turkey Zoo was forced to take down the sign that read 'Margaret The Killer Turkey' and initiated proceedings for the recovery of the €25,000 from Mike Joe on grounds of misrepresentation and fraud.

The subsequent High Court proceedings exposed Mike Joe's wrongdoing and he has been banned for life from rearing turkeys.

As for Margaret, well the Turks took a shine to the gentle Irish turkey because of her pleasant disposition and pleasing demeanour. Margaret has been placed in the ostrich enclosure and the biggest of birds have treated her as one of their own. And so Margaret will live for a good few Christmases to come.

The sheep killing continued even after Margaret emigrated to Turkey and the puma was shot. The guards solved the crime and the culprits were none other than the hunting dogs owned by several members of the sheep ranchers' posse who shot the puma.

There are those in the foothills who claim Mike Joe is now selling his illegal turkey growth substances to Tour de France cyclists, sundry weightlifters, assorted shot-putters and sprinters who finish fourth.

To my detractors I would say: how can you accuse me of writing about sex when the woman I am writing about, namely Mrs 39, hasn't had sex for 39 years, rising 40?

15

We're Keeping Mrs 39 On The Straight And Narrow — But What If Her 'Dead' Husband Returns?

March 23, 2019

IT'S been a while now since we brought you an update on the activities of The Woman Who Hasn't Had Sex for 39 Years.

Her affairs, or rather her lack of affairs, have engrossed the nation, and men in particular. Last time we told you her dead husband may have been seen shopping in New York.

There could be serious social welfare consequences. Mrs 39 may be forced to pay back 27 years of the widow's pension. More about the dead man walking later.

I am aware, and have been made aware, newspapers are no place for stories about sex. I was told if I keep on writing about Mrs 39, the Irish Independent will end up on the high-up shelves where 'Playboy' was kept. "Only basketball players will read the paper," warned our circulation department. To my detractors I would say: how can you accuse me of writing about sex when the woman I am writing about, namely Mrs 39, hasn't had sex for 39 years, rising 40.

So keep on reading if you are one of the moral minority. There's no fear of your being offended in any way. You might even get to find out about the newest news from the story of a latter-day Lazarus, who was Mrs 39's late husband. Personally I think he's dead, but so too did Doubting Thomas.

The reason I know for a fact Mrs 39 hasn't had the bit of sex since our last update is she would have told me so. Mrs 39 knows I'm thinking of writing a book about her life and times and she has been made aware (by me) if she did have the bit of sex my novel would be dead in the water.

Mrs 39 can do as she wishes. Her sex life is her own. But I did suggest, subtly, that if she had the bit of sex, I would have to hand back the advance I was given by the publishers, Ballpoint Press. The problem is that I have already spent the money.

I have to admit I did put a good few men off her in my role as gatekeeper. There isn't a week goes by that some lad doesn't present himself in John B's asking for an introduction.

The Monaghan chicken farmer asked me Mrs 39's age.

I always honour Mrs 39's two major anniversaries by giving her a card with a Lotto ticket inside. Mrs 39 has no interest in winning a large amount of money as she is afraid it might change her.

All she wants to do is to spin the wheel and I will tell you why later on. Her birthday is scheduled for April 30, which is the same date as last year when I was sent 57 bottles of perfume. Lads, please do not send any Chanel, Lolita Lempicka, or Issey Miyake this year.

Mrs 39 has 19 years' supply stockpiled and has taken to pouring perfume down the bowl as toilet freshener. Every time she flushes, her house smells like the entrance to Brown Thomas on Valentine's Day.

I told the suitor from Monaghan Mrs 39 was no spring

chicken. One of my great gifts as a barman is that I talk to people in their own language.

The chicken farmer told me he himself wasn't much gone the 60. He was well up for the date. "I didn't come all this way for nothing. We will make the feathers fly," he said.

The chicken farmer volunteered "to put Mrs 39 out of her misery".

I was annoyed. I admit that much. Things are so tough in the pub game right now. Us publicans have to put up with conversations we would never have listened to in the good times. As he was only drinking tea, I spoke my mind.

"Is it how you think," I said, "that women who have no interest in the other thing are automatically miserable?"

The chicken farmer was taken aback. To be fair to the man, he thought he was doing a good deed. "It was a Christian thing to do."

It's not that Mrs 39 hates all men just because her late husband went offside.

Mrs 39 is nearly gone broke from buying Lotto tickets.

She is mad about 'Winning Streak' presenter Marty Whelan, "but only as a friend".

Marty never met Mrs 39 and will only become aware of this platonic love when he reads this column.

Marty cracked one of his famous jokes last Thursday on Lyric. It went: "What did the traffic light say to the approaching car?" The answer: "Look away, I'm changing."

Mrs 39 hasn't stopped laughing since.

The poor woman needed cheering up. There have been several alleged sightings of her dead husband in New York.

He was said to have been seen mixing concrete on the

54th floor of a Manhattan high-rise. Mrs 39 was sure this wasn't true, as Mr 39 was afraid of heights.

Then, she added in, with a hint of bitterness: "He never worked a day in his life."

When Mrs 39 was happily married, during the first three days of the honeymoon, she described Mr 39's long nose as Roman. After he ran off with the younger woman, Mrs 39 referred to the nose as "a snout".

I asked the woman who spotted Mr 39 in Macy's to retract. Just to put Mrs 39 at ease. She agreed.

"Are you sure it was him?" I asked.

"I'm fairly certain. I noticed the nose," she replied.

But it was the walk, she went on. "He had a very distinctive but barely noticeable limp."

I asked Mrs 39 if her ex had a nice walk. She sighed.

"Oh yes, Billy, he had a very sexy walk. It was as if he was a cowboy after getting off a horse and he had a lovely bottom for Wranglers.

"He had one leg shorter than the other but that made him even more desirable."

And there she was looking off into the yonder of long ago, as if the dead man with the John Wayne gait was walking up William Street to greet her.

I'm worried now. What if he's still alive? We will have to start a GoFundMe page to pay back the pension.

And if Mr 39 ever comes back to Ireland, will Mrs 39 fall for him all over again?

16

What Ireland Needs Most In 2017 Is A Dedicated Ministry Of Sex

January 2, 2017

THE year is only a day old and already I've broken several New Year's resolutions. The first broken resolution was to refrain from writing about sex in 2017 on account of the fact it drives so many people mad.

But sex doesn't go away. It's always there. I gave in to myself. So here I am writing away about sex and the year barely run in.

Before we get to the sex, I promised the dietician I would try to eat broccoli, which is full of goodness, but I hate broccoli.

The next resolution was to go off the drink. New Year's Eve was a night for the hardy and the drinking spilled over in to January 1, which was the day I had planned to go on the dry.

Another broken resolution was to get my facts right. So there I was singing about Annie Moore from Ireland, who I explained in a lengthy introduction to the song "was the first person ever to check in at Ellis Island on the first of January and she was only 15 years".

Annie was 17 and Ellis Island opened on today's date which is not the first of January but the second.

We will go back to the sex. Here is our usual warning.

Please stop reading now if you are easily offended. There is graphic imagery in the rest of this piece which may upset certain persons. The word ride is mentioned at least twice. Don't say you weren't tipped off.

We will make concessions to sensibilities. There will be no mention of the word clitoris, the location of which is as much of a mystery to most Irishmen as the whereabouts of Lord Lucan. There's talk in tech circles of an app based on satnav technology to help with directions but that's a story for another day.

You always know you've upset people when the letters come in the post. Do not fret. No one in their right mind should take any notice of anything written by a newspaper columnist.

But when someone goes to the bother of writing a letter and licks it and posts it, you know they are up in arms. Usually, the anonymous letters are on the lines of 'there's no such thing as sex' which unfortunately seems to be the case for so many people in this country.

The letter writers will write to say there's nothing uplifting in this piece, as if this column is suffering from sort of literary erectile dysfunction. And what has the paper come to? There will be calls for a sacking.

I will mount a campaign, if you pardon the expression, in favour of more sex. Health Minster Simon Harris has steadfastly ignored all of my pleas for the establishment of a dedicated Ministry of Sex. Maybe he might engineer a deal with Fianna Fáil to establish a minimum number of rides per person a year. We could package the deal as an end to civil war politics. I don't know of anyone who has ever said he or she wasn't in the better of the bit of sex, so the health benefits are a given.

There will be savings off paying property tax, water

charges and USC. With extra points if you live in remote parts of rural Ireland, where women are scarce enough.

So for every time you have sex, there will be a reward like a free cappuccino or a discount on the amount of tax you are paying, if you hit big numbers.

It's like the ride-to-work scheme introduced by the Green Party. Now everyone owns a bike.

I know some of you will be upset by all this, even though I did warn you to stop reading right at the start of the sex talk. Bail out now. There's even more sex down the page and it's frank. I'm only guessing now but I'd say I'm bang on here when I write that people are upset because this proposal effectively pays people to have sex.

You will be saying he's turning the women of Ireland into whores and the men into gigolos. My reply is it is our patriotic duty on this, the first Monday in the 101st year after 1916, to have more sex for Ireland and not really for ourselves, in any selfish sort of way. Bank holiday Mondays are revolution days.

The savings to the Exchequer will be enormous. Even if you've gone off sex, get back on. Men and women died for Ireland. Now it's time to ride for Ireland.

There's no time like the present. Get at the sex straight away. Most of you are off work today. Spinning in the gym isn't half as much fun.

Sex can be a voyage of discovery and there are several places where the deed can be done such as in the hot press, which is a type of poor man's sauna, and the attic, which is a poor man's mile-high club.

More sex means less mental health problems as sex makes people happy. I read somewhere you can run off a burger and chips by having sex just the once, so there will be a massive cardiovascular dividend from all the exercise.

Lives will be saved but there will be fatalities. Go easy at the start. Your warm-up should involve lengthy foreplay with lots of stretching. Sedentary foreplay like ear-nibbling and the like isn't really cardio and should be discouraged.

For those men of you who are not that fit, it might be as well to have the sex on a hill or tilt the bed with the hind legs underpinned by useless books you got for Christmas. It's all about momentum.

Sex can be good too for arthritis and mobility if you venture beyond the traditional Irish favourite, the 'missionary position'. Try out more supple methods, such as are practised in the Indian sub-continent.

There are practical difficulties to be overcome, such as the actual administration of the more sex scheme. I would propose a system of self-assessment.

It just dawned on me just now that I did make the resolution about checking my facts. I'm not sure if having sex will get rid of all the burger and chips calories but you can always go again, to be on the safe side. Come to think of it, kale isn't as horrible as broccoli but it's bad enough all the same. We might leave that one until next year, which will be here before we know it.

17

Parents, If Your Son Or Daughter Is At College, There's More Than A 50pc Chance They're On Drugs

November 24, 2018

THERE is more money around and the recovery has reached rural Ireland. The improvements in terms of income are here at last, but in smaller increments than in the cities.

That is the good news, but the downside is our drug problem has reached epidemic proportions. There isn't a city, town or village that has not been overrun. The post offices are closing and the drug dealerships are opening up.

Yet nobody seems to know. There is hardly a mention of the epidemic in the media. The politicians are quite rightly concerned with the problem of homelessness.

The drug crisis dwarfs the homelessness crisis in terms of scale and the numbers affected. In fact, the drug epidemic feeds numbers in to the homelessness crisis. Brexit and the results thereof will affect Ireland forever, but right now the most pressing problem is drugs and our politicians on every side are downgrading the effects of the worst scourge since the Famine.

This may seem like hyperbole but I swear to you that I speak the truth. I also swear to you that I am absolutely

THE VERY BEST OF BILLY KEANE

sure of my facts. Please believe me, I beg of you, before it is too late.

I have spoken to addiction counsellors, gardaí, students and even a drug dealer.

But the most telling evidence comes from those who are using drugs on a regular basis.

The students I spoke to in UCD last weekend estimated that about 60pc of their friends are on drugs. The story in the other third-level institutions is equally depressing. The vast majority of young people are on drugs. If your son or daughter is under 30, the likelihood is he or she is taking drugs.

And I'm not talking about students here who are sitting around in their pyjamas smoking a rite-of-passage joint while watching 'Home and Away' on a wet afternoon.

The young are on hard drugs. There are heroin addicts in every town. I spoke to the chairperson of a GAA club who told me two of their best players, who could well have gone on to play for the county, are now registered heroin addicts.

I know of decent boys and girls who were targeted and duped. Their lives have been destroyed by the new breed of Black and Tans who are ruining our country. The ironic part of all this is the Irish Tans wrap themselves in the Tricolour and pretend to be republicans. They are criminals and traitors.

The effect of the drugs changes and ruins lives.

The experts are still not sure of the effects of some of the newer drugs being sold by the dealers. What we do know is the problems caused by drug use will have catastrophic consequences, not just now but for decades to come.

Show this piece to any young person and they will be in total agreement. I am that confident of the facts.

Gardaí I spoke to in seven different counties are overwhelmed.

They are in agreement with the 60pc figure.

One garda told me of a stag party and 23 out of the 27 on the stag were doing cocaine. They all had "good jobs" and came from "respectable families".

The Maurice McCabe case has seriously undermined public confidence in the Garda, even though only a small number were out to destroy Maurice.

One of the saddest parts of Katie Hannon's incredibly moving documentary was Maurice McCabe telling how proud he was when he first wore the Garda uniform, only to have his life destroyed by his colleagues.

One garda told me "the proudest day for any garda is when we throw our caps in the air in Templemore. My friend turned to me and said we're gardaí now and we shed a tear".

His friend was beaten up just a few months ago while he was trying to stop a drug-fuelled fight outside a night club.

The vast, vast majority of our gardaí joined because they wanted to make a difference; they cared and they were patriots in the service of the State.

They continue to put their safety on the line every time they go out to a crime scene. There isn't a garda in the country who hasn't been in a near-death situation. Not one.

There isn't a garda on the street who will disagree with a single word written here. Yet they feel they cannot speak out.

One garda said to me: "The people might think we are after overtime or on the make in some way."

Gardaí are under-manned, undermined, under-resourced and overwhelmed.

They just cannot keep up with the huge increase in drug use. There was always drugs, but in the course of a year the problem has become a crisis of epidemic proportions.

I have been reading the provincial papers a lot over the past five or six weeks.

The court cases in the newspapers are a telling reminder of just how low we have sunk as a nation.

The 'Tipperary Star', 'Waterford News and Star', 'Connacht Tribune', 'Donegal Democrat', 'Clare Champion', 'Laois Nationalist', 'Clonmel Nationalist', 'Dundalk Democrat' and 'The Kerryman', among many others, feature numerous court reports of drug offences or crimes committed because of drug use.

But the relatively recent rapid increase in drug sales has not yet been reported in any forensic or scientific manner for the very valid reason that it takes time to collect, collate and asses the data.

But if you want to know the up-to-date state of toxic play, just ask any student or any garda.

To parents, I would say if your son or daughter is studying in any of our third-level colleges, there is more than a 50pc chance he or she is on drugs.

And the young lad or girl who went off to college full of hopes and dreams in September may have already suffered irreparable damage to their mental and physical well-being.

18

One Book Was All It Took To Eliminate The Grey Out Of Middle-aged Sex

July 24, 2012

MACKENNA'S, our local hardware store, has run out of duct tape. Woulfe's book shop has sold out of '50 Shades of Grey'. These two events are not unconnected.

I have never read '50 Shades of Grey' and have no intention of so doing. I just couldn't face into hundreds of pages of bondage and worse again... romance. Anyway, until recently I was sure '50 Shades of Grey' was a hair dye from Just For Men.

This book, which I have never read, has ruined the lives of many poor men who are now worn out after a belated sexual awakening from their partners.

It has gone from one extreme to the other, an insider told me. "None at all and now this. A glut."

His eyes were set as far back in his head as those headlamps in sport cars. The broken one walked as if he was shouldering a sumo's coffin and the raw-red rings around his wrists told a story of handcuffs and nylon ties.

The weight is falling off him. He has taken to hiding out in the attic. His pet name for his wife used to be Yummy. Now it's Torquemada.

I didn't remember him having the bandy legs. Broken and forlorn, he trudges to the chemist for vitamin supplements, protein shakes, caffeine and Viagra. He throws the lot into a juicer and downs the cocktail in one gulp.

And what were the women of the world at during all those years before the book came out?

There they were lying in bed, that's what, completely turned off by the husband, with his beer belly and athlete's feet.

His idea of foreplay was to pull across the curtains and then our hero puts all of his very being into the lovemaking, for the full three minutes.

The afterplay comes next with snoring as she pulls the rim of her fit-all-sizes, double-gusset passion killers, elasticated below the knee, up over her fluff-filled belly button.

Ah but it didn't used to be like this. They were in love once and several times more than once in those lusty days of yore. Back from the honeymoon in Santa Ponsa, brown as berries and so much in love.

Over the threshold of their new home he carries her.

He used to rub baby oil into her back and nibble her ear like it was a stick of celery.

He's togging out with lads at that first match back after the honeymoon and as he takes off his shirt the full-back remarks "I see you went topless". He tells the team the hickey on his neck came from an insect bite.

The boys laugh loud and long when the manager says the insects in Santa Ponsa must be the size of sparrowhawks. He's embarrassed but kinda proud too.

But then young Mikey came along and then the twins. She's exhausted and with her focus divided in four parts, loses all interest. As they say around here "she let herself go", so much so strangers on the bus offer her a seat as they think she's expecting.

He, frustrated and hurt, visited a lap-dancing club in Manchester when he was over for a United game and squandered all his dosh on a six-foot blond from a country that used to be owned by Russia.

I have lost count of the amount of middle-aged men who tell me their wives have turned off sex completely. Maybe there should be a concerted national campaign from the HSE on sex education for the older man and woman.

But sure the Santa Ponsa Stud can't even say the word. It's called "the other thing" and if he broaches the subject with herself, all he gets is a "shut up you aul eeejit". What would the likes of us want with that carry on at our age?'

So many long-term relationships are passionless and celibate.

Back in the old days the lack of sex was blamed on the church. My dad put four of us through college by writing books about mountainy men who fell in love with rubber women.

But that was then and now the dearth continues. There has to be some underlying reason for the sexless relationships. Is it money, hormonal, lack of technique or just plain boredom?

The health professional I spoke to put it down to a lack of mutual understanding.

"Many women," she said, "have no idea how important sex is to men. Men must understand that foreplay does not start in the bedroom but is part of a process of nurturing, caring and connection.

"Younger women might just get ignited by the purely physical but as time goes on she'd be more likely to get intimate if he emptied the dishwasher and put out the bins."

"Is it a reward then for being a good boy?" I ask.

"Yes in a way and this comes out in the book. He looks after her -- the heroine."

Thin, fit people are also in the total abstinence hell. There are thousands upon thousands who live lies of lives and how sad is that? I just know it anecdotally from talking over the counter.

Bar talk can be deadly serious. Funny and cruel at the same time.

The malevolent man was out to maim.

"I hear X is knocking off your wife."

There was a stunned silence and then the jilted husband answered: "Sure that's one less job for me to do."

Affairs are on the up. In every walk of life.

The lack of sex in mature relationships is a world pandemic and that's why '50 Shades' has outsold the 'Bible'.

We have only scratched the surface here. The issue has to be opened up for public debate. Health Minister James Reilly must act, and now.

It's time for an Irish Kinsey report into all aspects of this 21st Century famine.

In the meantime, wheel out that bin and bring the milk in from the gate as you're at it. There's nothing worse than a love life gone sour.

19

An Post Should Deliver More — Not Less — For Rural Ireland

September 17, 2018

AN Post are closing down 159 post offices in rural Ireland. But this is only a minor event according to An Post.

The good news is a bare 3.7% of the customers will be affected. Whew! Gee, what a relief. Ah sure that's not too bad. The 3.7 seems so small and teeny and would you miss it that much?

I was never great at the sums. Had to repeat mata in Babies. The answer to the next hard sum is cogged. So let's see what happens if 3.7% of the population, as opposed to customers, were to be affected? Does that sound reasonable? The answer is 176,601 which might not be too far out when it comes to guessing the impact of the cuts.

An Post claim every place with a population of over 500 people will be guaranteed a post office. This depends on your definition of a place. An Post stopped counting at the speed limits on the roads, in and out of the villages.

This approach is restrictive and narrow. The living lands of rural Ireland are based on the parish system. The parish rather than the village is the place that should have been counted up. Take for example Ballylongford here in North Kerry. Bally the village has a population of 392. Twenty years ago Bally had more than 500 people living in the village. But Bally the parish has enough of a population for nearly three post offices.

Bally the parish is the catchment area for the football team, and this is the natural definition of place and homeland all over Ireland. An Post picked their own borders.

To be fair, An Post did flag these closures some years ago and we pleaded here for people to support their local post offices. But many didn't lift a finger to back their own.

The Post Master from the west tried his best to increase business. Post offices are paid according to the amount of transactions processed. The Post Master knew An Post were about to offer him a severance or retirement package. He was torn between loyalty to his community and the need for some money to see him through his oldest years.

The Postmaster even went to the local parish priest. The good priest, as most of them are, delivered a sermon to the effect that the parishioners should collect their social welfare and pensions from the local post office rather than go on line. He also mentioned T.V. and dog licenses, savings accounts, as well as the children's allowance.

"What would it take", he said, "only the bare few minutes, once a week". But only one new customer came in to the post office and that person was a relative of the Post Master. The Post Master took the package.

I would not blame any post office owner for taking the deal. This was a last resort and a terrible emotional turmoil for the Post Masters and Post Mistresses.

I wrote here about the country publican who told us

the people who moaned most when the local pub shut down were those who never came in.

The government must intervene. I believe they will cave in to some extent. An Post's methodology is fatally flawed but I can understand the position of An Post. They were charged with making a profit. An Post will change the future of rural Ireland. Financial people are always more comfortable closing things down. It's the easy way out.

So here's how it works. The government pass on the job of closing the post offices to An Post, who in turn put the heat on the Post Masters to close up, or die through cuts and slashes.

An Post must treat this problem on a case by case basis. It may well be there is no one interested in taking over a rural post office. Fair enough, but new blood and new ideas can revive this priceless asset to places already half-beaten. This is about morale more than money. This is about people and yes, profit too.

The Bottom Liners, as ever, take a narrow view. There is a human cost never shown on the balance sheets. Older people have been forgotten. It's as if the big corporations can't wait for them to die. There are those who do not own cars or live in places where smoke signals are more effective than broadband. What will they do?

Who will the lonely talk to now that the shops, post offices and pubs are gone? The Bottom Liners did not cost the lack of hope. Mental health has been discounted as a zero. The Bottom Liners are blinkered by their training and the conventions of a failed system of accounting. Sociologists should have an input to all public accounts. Local accountants who know the area should be asked for their view. The Bottom Liners have failed us time and again. Their pixels wouldn't fill a car mirror.

There has to be hope. There has to somewhere to cling to, a door open for business, somewhere to laugh and somewhere to cry. We need a rallying place for the resistance.

Let An Post ask for submissions and bids from those who are interested in taking over the lost post offices. The government must lay it on the line. They must if necessary provide financial support.

Fianna Fail must make their backing of the budget conditional on saving the post offices. I understand that in some cases An Post may be open to accepting an alternative site, but these are far and few between in an Ireland sadly lacking in infrastructure.

There is an alternative in Ballylongford but An Post have not given any guarantees. My cousin is the local councillor. Liam Purtill is Fine Gael and he has written to several minister for help. Says Liam "this is the last straw."

Fianna Fail's Jimmy Moloney is fully behind the restoration of the North Kerry post offices. The political parties are united for once.

The O'Rahilly was a Ballylongford man who charged a British machine gun in 1916. He was one of the finest kind of patriots. The O'Rahilly didn't even want the rebellion to go ahead. He knew Easter 1916 was doomed, but he fought anyway. Did The O'Rahilly die to have the post office closed down in the place he loved so well? Well did he? And did he go on-line to die?

The O'Rahilly died in a hail of machine gun fire, very close to the GPO, where the decision was made to close down the post office in his beloved Ballylongford.

20

Farewell To My Friend Fr Pat — A Man First And Then A Priest, Always With A Twinkle In His Eye

May 6, 2017

I TRACED my fingers along the worn limestone flags at St Batt's Holy Well while my friend Fr Pat Moore was being laid to rest over the road in old Aghavallen.

He was a man for all reasons, a man for all seasons. Pat died from cancer but it never killed his faith or his spirit. He went through some doubting days and sad days. He was one of us, you see. One of you, and one of me. A man first and then a priest.

To be made in to a saint from one of us, miracles are needed. Moore, as we called him at school, performed his miracle. Just one, but it was a big one. He was lovely to everyone.

His miracle was like St Brigid's cloak. St Brigid asked for a site to build a monastery in Kildare and the cynical chieftain agreed to give her as much land as her cloak would cover. Brigid threw the small cloak on the grass and it stretched out over hundreds of hectares. Moore covered so much ground and made so much out of so many. His blogs beat time and distance. He was inclusive and wrote as he spoke.

"It didn't matter who you were, or what you were. He

had time for everyone." So said a man who had nothing, bar Moore and his rosary beads.

In the end, Fr Pat was a kind of a modern-day martyr. All that giving took its toll. He wore out. The good priest didn't know how to say the word "no", but he was mad for tea and talk. It was his call.

Fr Pat was the one who said: "We do death very well in Ireland." And we do. He got a great send-off. The scholar loved the bit of Latin and he loved the serene. The parting was in his likeness.

If Moore was a lake and a meteor dropped in to it from outer space, there wouldn't be so much as a ripple. He was calm and giving, funny and spiritual. He never killed the boy most men stifle. When we met, we got giddy, like we did all those years ago in St Michael's. I have come to the realisation my old school friend is still with us. By coincidence I was in our school on the day he was buried. I had the old class in my eye and where we all sat.

I got to thanking him. The abuse cases and the failure to embrace gay people turned me off the Church. I am all for women priests. Pat was too. Women loved him and he loved the company of women.

Every now and then he would casually, accidentally on purpose, drop in a story of great goodness or spirituality in the course of our conversations. He won me over when mam was dying. Thanks Pat. Tell her to keep an eye on me.

Moore had so many causes, so many cases to deal with. He managed to be one thing to all men, and that was compassionate. Fr Pat was a great scholar but he always managed to distil his hours of thinking in to one simple, meaningful sentence. Moore always resisted the temptation to show off how much he knew.

Sometimes I would steal his sermons, with his OK, and I often got a whole column out of one of his stories. Every now and then I supplied him with "joke of the day" as I had been doing steadfastly since we were 12. There was a "joke of the day" at Mass every Sunday in Duagh. Moore was pure box office. The bells rang out 'Danny Boy' for the emigrants. He was a man of his own people. But he was a priest too. There were over 50 at his funeral. Most of them I know, and they are good men, who do their best to perform the miracle of the cloak on a daily basis.

I met a grandmother, a mother and a daughter at his funeral Mass. The little girl cried for him until her eyes were red. One man, who suffered from the nerves, said to me: "If Fr Pat thought enough of me to keep on calling out to the house, even when I was a bit off, well then I must be some use, mustn't I?"

I was about to go to see my friend on the day he died, last Monday. The story I had for him was about the two lovely Lebanese sisters who called in to the pub that very morning. The Lebanese ladies told me their mother had two outfits in the basement of her apartment in New York. One was in case she died in the summer, and the other was in case she died in the winter. He'll love that, I thought. And then the word came through.

Moore too was getting ready. The Irish are like the Pharaohs. And I'll tell you how he made his preparations later on down the page.

Pat told me he couldn't cry when his mother died and it bothered him. Moore loved his mom so much, and he was very good to her when she fell into bad health. Pat cried for his mom before he died. He didn't have time for himself until near the very end. There's a priestly veneer and he discarded that. He opened up. Fr Pat wrote to me a couple of weeks ago. It was private but in the end I think he was ready.

Just before Christmas, we met up by accident. We

leafed through his plans for death. Pat wrote a book. It was his way of getting ready and of getting us ready. "It needs more," I said. "You have so much more to say." He replied: "That's as much as I can do." I knew then.

He wrote so beautifully. All 5,000 copies of 'Weathering a Storm' were sold. Moore, the great communicator, wanted to leave some of him for us when he was gone. There's a line or two where he says his friend Billy advised him to go to St Batt's to trace his fingers along the old stones where his people walked and prayed. "And ask the ancestors to re-ordain me in all that is life giving."

So happy I was to be called his "friend". And for all of you who feel the one of you can do so little to help others, Pat asks: "How many wells does it take to make a river? One, if it's big enough."

Here's the last "joke of the day" from the man himself. My friend was not capable of delivering a sermon without at least one laugh. He wrote about meeting a man who had cancer. Pat told him his story and he knew the man was going to ask about the prognosis. "To deflect him, I decided to be as bold as himself, and ask where he had it," Pat said. "His face and chest filled with air and joy collectively."

"Down there," he pointed, "in the playground area!" Only Moore could knock a laugh out of cancer. I turned back and kissed him on the forehead the last time we met. It was goodbye.

But I believe he is still with us. I believe he was there with me at St Batt's Well on Thursday when I traced my fingers along the grainy old weathered limestone, just as he had done a few months ago, here in this place of some peace.

21

One Year Has Passed And I Still Get The Urge To Ring Páidí

December 14, 2013

THE Kerry team were young and very nervous. It was 1997 and we hadn't won an All-Ireland since 1986. It was the morning of the final against Mayo.

He called the players to one side in the grounds of Blackrock College where the kickabout took place. I snuck over. He spotted me. Said nothing. It was just PO and the players. Maybe he knew, some day, I'd write about it.

At the time, I was a minor functionary in his backroom team. The talk is secret. That is the rule. All I can say is there was no shouting or roaring. It was a calm talk, but after that last few words there was no player in the group who didn't know exactly what his job was. There was no player who didn't know exactly what it meant to wear the green and gold.

"Are you alright?" he asked. "I'm fine," I said. The tears were coming down my face. "Was it alright?" he asked. I couldn't answer. Kerry won the most important All-Ireland ever. Páidí Ó Sé saved Kerry football. He had great men with him as selectors and the planner Seamus Mac-Gearailt kept us all grounded, but only Páidí could have won that All-Ireland.

This was Páidí at his best -- in control and beating the demons. There was a chaotic side to him too. Usually when there was drink involved.

It was the snowy January of '97 and I was at Cork Airport without a ticket. Páidí asked me to come on a trip with the Kerry team to the Canaries. I'm not sure what my job was -- and I'm still not sure. Páidí forgot all about asking me to go. Eventually, I travelled under the name of Bernie O'Callaghan. No one bothered to check my passport in the pre-9/11 times.

I blamed PO for two days, then one night he sent me over a drink and a note, it said we're going for walk tomorrow "to discuss tactics". There wasn't a word about tactics, but along with Eamonn Breen we had the funniest day ever. He knew all the Africans selling sunglasses by name. Their life stories. They knew him. And PO invited them all to Ventry. Jobs and beds for everyone. They sold him a pair of sunglasses the size of saucepans. We told him they were lovely.

You could never fall out with PO. Never. No matter what, because he'd always make it up to you. If you had a puncture outside his front door, it would be very hard to get him to take an interest -- but if your heart was breaking, he'd do all he could to fix it. My old friend was a mind doctor and he had a lovely counter-side manner.

In the end, his own heart broke down because it was too souped up to fit in a human frame and he drove himself too hard.

There were times when I used to feel awful for him. To be Páidí 24 hours a day -- especially in the summer -- was impossibly exacting. Everyone wanted a piece of him.

He was shy, you know. It was his first day in St Michael's in Listowel. PO was 18 and nervous. There wasn't a word out of him. Three months later, we'd have died for him. Our tiny school won all around us that year. Didn't lose a game. We won the Kerry Colleges for the first time ever. Our trainer John O'Flaherty was a football genius and he said some day Páidí would manage Kerry. I was 16 and I knew some day Páidí would win loads of All-Irelands.

Tommy O'Connell and myself walked home with Páidí every evening. There were so many yarns. They were the best days I had with him. When people left him alone, before he was famous, and he didn't have to be Páidí.

I remember bursting into the old man's study one evening, firing the schoolbag in the corner and telling him "I have no life". That was after the walk home, listening to Páidí's outrageous yarns, after a trip to London with the Kerry team.

He could be a meticulous planner and there was never a better fundraiser. His lovely family are keeping up the tradition. They raised thousands for heart equipment and the Páidí Ó Sé Tournament, now in its 25th year, takes place next February. The nephews are behind it too and I'd say PO is fierce proud. There's no better weekend anywhere. He was mad about Maire and the kids. PO wasn't your conventional father. There were times when he was put in the bold corner by his girls. Classic role reversal it was. He never chastised his kids. It was all love, funny one-liners, wisdom, holidays, walks, cycles and a soft-spoken gentleness you'd never think he had in him if you watched him playing football.

A couple of weeks ago, I was in bad form. I started to dial 066 915... then it dawned on me. Now, when you'd go ringing PO there wouldn't be a response like "I'll share your pain, man," or "I love you, bro". He wasn't exactly your modern man.

He hated bad news. So the best thing to do was just

THE VERY BEST OF BILLY KEANE

call him. He'd know from the tone of your voice if the treatment was needed. Then he'd get it going. There would be enough laughter to cure any pain.

He's dead a year tomorrow. Most of all I miss watching that brilliant mind thinking. You could see him winding up. Just to give a bit of himself. It was as if there was an empty thought bubble, like they have in the comics, waiting to be filled up and you would never quite know what he'd come out with.

I see him now in his new going-away-from-home suit with a tie knot as a big as an apple. There's a shine off him and he's as fit as a trout. I can still hear his legacy podcasts in my head.

And I always will.

22

Old Dreamers In Stands Still Rocking To Sleep With Visions Of Glory

February 8, 2014

THE curse of the crows woke me just before the dawn. The bedroom skylight is directly under their flight path from the rookery of the Parson's Wood to the scavenging lands.

Crows are like bar-room drunks. They raucously announce their every thought to all within earshot. Yes, I had a dream, and it came from that map Google will never track, in the tangled web where old thoughts meet new imaginings in the underworld under the cranium.

The dream was a young boy's dream of yesterday, today and tomorrow.

Picture us, the boy and the man, long ago, when as Dylan Thomas wrote 'there were wolves in Wales'. My father was six feet tall but back then I was sure he was 10ft 2ins. So off we went in the slow train, just the two of us, to Dublin, for the big game between Ireland and Wales.

Ireland were no-hopers and Wales were playing for the Grand Slam, with possibly the greatest backline of all time.

Ireland, then as now, were the best team for surprises. Ken Goodall, our young No 8, gathered a loose ball well out the field. Ken kicked ahead over the advancing Welsh. There was a foot race to the line. Goodall won the chase. Try for Ireland. I stood on the seat to see when the crowd jumped up. My father hoisted me up to 10' 2". I could see a smiling Goodall running back to the half-way line and all the lads were clapping him on the back.

We won 14-0 and I was hooked on rugby forever. So it is 40 years or so later, I'm still dreaming a small boy's dreams of glory. Yes, I was playing for Ireland against Wales this morning when the commuting crows cawed the premature full-time whistle on the occasion of my 10,000th cap.

We were fortunate to be in Cardiff for two real Grand Slams. My abiding memory on the night Wales beat us to win The Slam were the thousands of flattened plastic glasses under feet in Mary Street.

The crunch was like breaking the thin sheet of ice over winter puddles. No one, not even us, their cracked Celtic brothers and sisters, celebrate a rugby triumph with such unconfined, hedonistic joy.

There was our first Grand Slam in 61 years, when the delighted President McAleese presented the cup. The choreographing of the pack by Peter Stringer, the Ronan O'Gara winning drop-goal, and the last kick near miss by the Welsh are as much a part of our national treasure trove as gold crosses found in sods of turf.

Our neighbours from Wales own a golden treasury. This could be a three-in-a-row season for them. The Welsh travel in their thousands. Many will watch the match in Wexford Town this weekend. Their stirring and soulful anthems will be heard as far away as Dublin. It would not surprise us in the least if the much smaller Welsh force out-sang us in our own ground. The Welsh take their singing so seriously and treat every note and every word with respect and care.

The game could come down to a moment of brilliance. The plot is nicely thickened like a winter stew. St David is the patron saint of Wales, yet the Welsh backs are the Goliaths. The Irish will have to knock the big men down. It's easier to climb a fallen tree and the ferocity of the exchanges on the ground will determine the result. Fast ball for Wales could be disastrous for Ireland.

Wales looked heavy-legged against Italy and I have a feeling we will be helped by the weather. Even the skilful Welsh backs will find difficulty in battling the forecast gales and rain. I believe we can win if we get the breaks.

I witnessed a young boy dream in a suburban back garden on Orwell Road and I saw him kick a ball up against the back wall of his Nana's under the crows' flight path.

The boy plays at 10 today for his beloved Ireland. It's a big job when you're the dreamcatcher for a couple of million but this is where the boy always wanted to be. Dreams do come true.

I can feel it now. I can't wait to get going on the road to Dublin to savour the day and the trimmings. Are we there yet?

Will the story of today remain in our consciousness when time thieves memory? The child we all try so hard to repress renews us. Keeps us true.

The small boys reverie is of what will be, we dream of what was but somewhere in between there is a meeting.

So let our kids dream on. Tell the bed-time stories of old and new glories. And pray that when our children are old and dozy, their slippers will grow studs. For dreaming boys make for dreaming old men.

We need a new patriotism.
Ireland needs minders and
carers, dreamers and doers.
Dream and do. Dream and do.

23

Remember To Take Care, For The Days Can Become Years Before You Know It — Even In A Republic Of Opportunity

November 18, 2017

T HE following was a speech given by Billy Keane at a graduation class at the School of Health and Social Science Nursing and Health Care Studies and Social Sciences in Tralee, Co Kerry

'WELL you're here now, in gowns and hats. All dressed up and everywhere to go. Congratulations.

Congratulations in Kerry is "fair play to you". We say that if someone achieves something of note, so turn to the person next to you, shake his or her hand and then say "fair play to you".

Today is an end, but it is also a beginning. You will be the ones who take care of us in the years to come. You are the ones who will mind Ireland. Mind the humanity in yourselves and in others. Look after our beloved country. This is your stated aim and your quest. We need a new patriotism. Ireland needs minders and carers, dreamers and doers. Dream and do. Dream and do.

That little rolled up piece of paper you are about to receive isn't given out easily. It will go up on the wall now and it will be there forever.

THE VERY BEST OF BILLY KEANE

When you are old and full of sleep, many years from now you will say "was that me? Did I graduate from IT Tralee in November 2017?" Savour your day in this thriving college. I was at one of these graduations a few years ago and a young girl threw her hat in the air, rolled up her scroll into a paper bugle, and blew a loud yaaaahoo. No one can ever take this day from you.

Your loved ones are with you and they are as proud as could be. They too have played their part. Some of you were driven here by your parents, the very same parents who brought you to junior infants.

There will be days when you will be just as scared and lost as I was at four, when I started out for school. My mother wore a mini-skirt back in an Ireland when women dressed in long black shawls. There was an old boy who came into the pub and he said "Bill, if a man caught a glimpse of a woman's ankle in the old days, he'd be in a bother all day long". The builders whistled at my mam and I was mortified, so every day from then on I walked to school on my own.

Women didn't go to college back then.

To the women who have graduated here today I would say you owe it to those who came before you to stand up for your rights. To the men I would say stand up for the women. Back each other up.

Some of you took up college later on in life. Back when you were 18 maybe you weren't ready for learning, or maybe you couldn't afford to go, or maybe you had to raise kids, but now you are here because you want to be here. Your achievement is the best of all.

Many of you will go on to save women and men from death and pain, both physical and mental.

For you are now members of the caring professions. Giving and caring can be draining. Mind yourselves.

You will not be able to do your best for others if you don't take care of yourself.

And more of you will travel. That piece of paper is a passport to everywhere. Go abroad to learn, and earn. If you do good anywhere to anyone, you do good everywhere to everyone. But make the plan to come home on the day you leave, or many of you will never come back. Don't drift. Days become years before you know it. Ireland is a land of opportunity. Do not be put off by the constant stream of negativity. Fix what needs fixing, but try always to pick out the good in our country. We are a nation who care and take care. We are funny and open. We talk, we laugh and we cry. This is now an Ireland where we champion diversity and inclusion. To the new Irish here today, I say welcome and well done. We are all the one.

My mother passed away about two years ago. I miss my mam every day more than I can say. I was just thinking what advice she would give to me now if I was a young lad of 21 on graduation day. It might be "don't drink too much" and, "Bill, do not under any circumstances pose for a selfie with a woman by the name of FiFi." Be careful. Don't go too mad tonight. And if you take pics or video, ask permission first.

Yes, I have had my bad days, but do you know that sometimes disasters are no more than a change of direction when you are blown off course. You too will have set-backs and there will be times when maybe the world may seem like it is about to overcome and overwhelm you.

By getting to where you are today you have proven you can survive and thrive. Nothing in education is ever wasted. Make use of your knowledge and, more importantly, your knowledge of how to access the truth.

Study the politics of our country as diligently as you have studied to get that piece of paper that will prove you were here today on November 3, 2017.

Look behind the one-line lie on Facebook and the devious Twitter feed. Forensically examine every word. Lies become fake truth when lies are allowed to be repeated uncontested. Do not become the exploited or the duped, be the educators and the explainers. Be the ones who are in the know. Be the ones who serve the truth. Be yourselves and be true to yourselves.

There will be times when you will be overworked, under resourced and under paid. Fight for your rights by all means. But never forget how you feel today. Never lose the idealism and the love. Keep that sense of wonder you had in babies class. Keep on learning. Forever.

And lads, give the oul fella a kiss.

I only ever kissed my dad twice when I became an adult. He was a good old dad, a loving old dad, and when I came in home after being away for a while, we showed our affection by giving each other a few shoulders, like the way hurlers and footballers greet subs when they run on to the pitch.

That was the way it was back then. But dad kissed me the day I graduated. He was so proud and the next time I kissed him was when he was dying.

So show the love, men, and show it often and always. Talk, talk, talk. Keep nothing in. There's a cure in talk, boys.

As I was telling ye, my mam passed away two years ago. I was a bit like Prince Charles up to then, I didn't' do very much and I was very good at it.

It was August 30 last, a big birthday for me and I just couldn't go in to my first home. The day my mother died, our old home became a business. My mother would be there with the card and the kiss on every birthday.

There were 80 tourists on the way and I knew I might lose a good contract if I didn't open up. I tried to put the key in the lock but I couldn't. I just stood there frozen, with the tears in my eyes.

I'll go back nearly 50 years. My dad was upstairs writing 'The Field'. It nearly drove him crazy, trying to get inside the head of a murderer.

My mom was in the tiny kitchen, minding us, and making the dinner. The bell rang in the pub. I was sent out. I was a bar man at nine years of age and as you can see I haven't progressed very much in life ever since.

The football game in the hall was full on. We called it Hall Ball. There was no let up.

"Get out there Bill," urged my mam. I was playing football with my brothers who turned into two Kerry minors and we were laying into each other. I was boiling with the temper. "Get out there Bill. Shop face Bill, shop face."

Out I went into the pub, making small talk. "How's your cystitis, Mrs Murphy?" I ask. "And what would you like to drink, Mr Murphy?" That sort of thing.

The shop face becomes your real face, almost surreptitiously or subconsciously. The good form sneaks up on us unbeknownst.

So on August 30 last when I was frozen at the front door, I heard my mam's voice. "Shop face. Shop face, Bill." I put the key in the door and got on with my day.

I know for a fact the old man is still around because sometimes I get this unaccountable thirst. Not only did I inherit a pub, but I inherited a thirst as well.

Go forth now and multiply your knowledge. And don't forget the shop face. Do good wherever you go, and good will come to you.

Good luck to you all."

> *The news of The Old Stager's comeback does not go down well. He hasn't played for years. His belly is roundy and well established. There is no public response to his announcement.*

24

'Old Stager' Takes The Reins To Stop Booleen Boasting For Another Year

January 25, 2014

'ALRIGHT so," says The Old Stager, "I'll make my comeback." Men drink deep and are silent. The only sound in the packed pub is the cracking and spitting of the logs in the hearth.

The news of The Old Stager's comeback does not go down well. He hasn't played for years. His belly is roundy and well established. There is no public response to his announcement.

Soon, the hum builds back up, and in quiet corners there are whisperings and mutterings. The Old Stager takes no notice. He's forever young. Home he goes and does 20 push-ups before he goes to bed. His missus takes a peep out from under the duvet and pretends she's asleep.

The GAA season is about to get going. The Old Stager gets to thinking about his place in the world. The inter-county lads have been at it for a while now. Wouldn't it be lovely to win one last championship he thinks. One more year. One more trip to the old national school with the cup.

The Old Stager rummages around the hot press for his togs and boots. The togs wouldn't fit around his thumb now, seven years on since he last kicked a ball. The boots are as hard as the road. There are stony ridges and crevices from lace to toe. He puts them down to boil in the big pot used to cook the ham at Christmas.

The Old Stager puts off going for the six-mile run he planned late last night. The back is in spasm from the 20 press-ups. The three kids under three have been up since 6.00am. How is he going to find time to train twice a week with a match every Sunday? Herself is working hard enough to provide for the family as it is. Herself is just back from the gym. "What's that smell?" she asks. Steam rises from the ham pot. The boots are done.

Herself is about to explode. But then she stops. He hadn't the price of a new pair and he's afraid or too proud to ask her for the money. There's no building going on. She plans to call her brother to see if there are plasterers needed. She sheds a little tear, changes her mind and makes another call instead. To the club captain.

You'd wonder how The Old Stager will cope with the black card. He played it hard, but fair. He was never one for blackguarding young lads. For a while he worries he might turn in to one of those so called 'hard lads,' who try to make up for lack of pace by taking the heads off opponents.

The Old Stager thinks about it. He'd hate to turn into one of 'dem lads.' The black card might not be such a bad thing he thinks. He'd be safe from young lads out to make a name for themselves by taking easy scalps, like his.

The lads down in the pub have a name for the black card already. The 'tenna clubs' they're calling it. The worst card in the deck for 25 or 31.

The black fills in the sky. Still no run. No gym either. There's a knock at the door. Out he goes. The lads are there. All the lads bar the college lads and the lads working in the city.

"Come in," he says. "What's up?" he asks. He knows well why they are here. It's to ask him not to come back. It was a mad notion anyway. Brought on by drink and a yearning to be someone again. He's the 'tenna clubs' now. The Old Stager will say the back is gone and he was only seeing if he was up to it anyway.

The lads sit on the shoulders of sofas and armchairs. The good room is full. The captain clears his throat like the lad calling out 'testing 1, 2, 3' on a mike at the AGM. The lads stop talking.

"We want you to train the team this year? There's no one the lads would like more. It was unanimous to ask you," says the captain.

"As is in a player-coach?" asks The Old Stager. "Not exactly," replies the captain. "We know you'd be well able for it, but with the demands of the modern game and all that and what with being in Division 4C this year, we'll need a coach who will be focused entirely on the one job."

The modern game and all that. Sure isn't managing Tooreenganbonniv nearly harder than Manchester United, such is the weight of public expectation.

The Old Stager is teary. "I'm honoured lads. Truly honoured. Tooreenganbonniv is in my blood. I'm not sure, though, what with three small babbies and all that and Herself working nights. I'll need time to talk to her. I'd say now it is just a few years too soon."

Herself comes in from the kitchen with the first of several plates of sandwiches and a big pot of tea. "Go for it," she says. "Go on. You can't let the lads down. It's been seven years since Tooreenganbonniv last won the championship. We'll never stick listening to dem Booleen boys boasting for another year."

The new coach and his players talk long in to the night. Plans are made and the future is bright. When the lads are all gone home The Old Stager asks Herself. "How did you get the sandwiches ready so quick?" "What sandwiches?" she asks. He gives her a little squeeze. "Thanks".

25

Donal's Video A Powerful Reminder Of His Vital Quest

October 14, 2013

DONAL WALSH'S last video is a poem and a prayer for the living, the forsaken and the almost broken.

He was there in the bright early summer in his own home at the foot of the mountains, on the edge of the sea by the banks of a canal.

In the place he loved best, shining out at us with his wavy brown hair, the handsome boyish face and the big, brown conker eyes.

Donal knew his life was ebbing fast.

He wanted to be told and his parents made sure. They knew him better than anyone. Knew he needed to know because Donal had things to do. Things to say. Quests to make and lives to save.

He was just a boy, like any other boy. So we must see him as one of his own gang. His own generation. Just a boy.

The new video clip produced by the HSE is very short but very powerful.

Donal's first raw interview hit home. Suicide rates dropped but time thieves away the strength of the message.

We forget.

Millions of images come at us every day. Space is filled in the editing suites in our heads and older stories make way for new clips.

The all too sad pattern is starting up again. Our teenagers are dying from suicide. Donal's father Fionbarr praises the courage shown by the parents of school girl Chloe Kinsella, who died by suicide last week in Limerick. "It was," he says, "like Donal was whispering on my shoulder. The priest said the family, in the depth of their grief, asked that the funeral would not be a glorification of suicide and they wanted the young people to choose to live life.

"Chloe's parents had the courage to continue the conversation Donal started."

With Fionbarr and Elma's permission we have re-arranged his spoken goodbyes, line under line in the form of the poem.

Elma hopes her young lad's message will get through.

"When our teenagers see how weak Donal was physically and how his voice was beginning to go and how much of an effort it was for him, we hope they will listen. It took so much out of Donal to make the video. But he wanted to do it."

Donal wrote his epitaph through a journey of weeks rather than the years most of us get, but he was also travelling to some sort of a state of grace.

Maybe it's just me and part of our innate human longing for some sort of sign there is another life, a hereafter. A place to meet those we have lost or those we are leaving behind. This is the big question of our time, or any other age.

Donal's thinking was clear, even if the frail body was giving up on him.

It was as if Donal had help from a higher power and that in some way your God and mine was speaking through the teenager from Blennerville.

And so we have formed the opinion that young Donal's last poem was made half-way between heaven and here.

> We happened to be in London on the day in 1990 when Mrs Thatcher was 'stabbed in the front' by her own party and was sacked as prime minister. People danced in the streets.

26

Maggie Caused Much Heartache But It's Time To Bury Her Deeds

April 15, 2013

I WAS standing at the gates of the cordoned off Downing Street when there was a flurry of activity. "What's up?" we asked the policeman who stood at the top of the street.

"Mrs Thatcher is dead," he said.

So I was at Number 10, more or less, when the Iron Lady died of a stroke in The Ritz Hotel. Not a tear was shed at her old street. In the distance the prime minister or someone important was making a statement. We leaned over to get a better look. The policeman waved us back. He apologised with a "sorry mate."

We happened to be in London on the day in 1990 when Mrs Thatcher was 'stabbed in the front' by her own party and was sacked as prime minister. People danced in the streets.

It was a pound a pint in the Bogside in Derry last Monday night. Some criticised the celebrations. The truth is Mrs Thatcher had blood on her hands. The Provos were accessories, but the Iron Lady was mainly responsible for the terrible and painful deaths of the hunger strikers. She refused to grant minor give-ins that are now standard practice. For the hunger strikers, it was about being allowed concessions such as family visits.

Mahatma Gandhi wrote: "The weak can never forgive. Forgiveness is the attribute of the strong." The hunger strikers were young and in poor health with all sorts of pressures heaped upon them. Yes, they were men of violence but they, too, were victims of time and place. Mrs Thatcher was the strong one and she didn't have the humanity or the wisdom to forgive.

It was a fine Monday morning in London when she died. Flags were quickly lowered to half-mast and Londoners got on with their daily lives. The defining events in our lives are always present in our consciousness. Yet within a few years these watersheds trickle into history for all but those of us who lived in such times. I began to wonder, what was it all for?

The young lad working in the coffee stall asked his boss "what did Mrs T do that made her so famous?"

"Fell out with the whole bloody world," replied the older cockney.

The TV crews were setting up across the road from the Houses of Parliament. More flags at half-mast, Big Ben chimed his loudest at midday and Mrs T barely dead a half-an-hour. A well-dressed politician wearing a black tie strode by imperiously. He just had to be a Tory.

The Japanese newly-weds were posing for a photograph outside Westminster Abbey. She was petite, almost like a doll. He was a little lad in a boy-band jacket, skinny jeans and glitter on his hair.

The best man looked as if he was taking time off from his waiting job. The bridesmaid was shy and very beautiful. She had to be cajoled into standing in for the pictures.

"Did you get married in Westminster Abbey?" I asked the bride.

"I wish," she said.

The best man asked: "Why all the TV crews?"

Mrs Thatcher is dead, we told him.

"Who?"

None of them had ever heard of her here in the patch she ruled for so many years. Thatcher's England is no more. And again I asked myself, what was it all for?

She wasn't a humanitarian by any stretch. Mrs Thatcher organised her own funeral. She was controlling, right to the end. The ceremony will take place on Wednesday in St Paul's Cathedral after a parade through London. She will be buried next to her husband, Denis.

We have peace now in the North. But history is like psychotherapy. Old wounds are re-opened and past grievances are revisited. The end aim is a cure, but Mrs Thatcher has caused more heartache than any other democratic leader of her time.

Britain, to her credit, has now made friends with most of Mrs Thatcher's enemies but there are those who will dig up her sins to further their own campaigns. It is too soon for revisionism. We are getting on far too well with the British now to risk going back to the bad old days. As a country, and more especially as a people, the British like us very much. I often get the impression we are their favourite foreigners. Let's just move on quickly then. For now.

When she is buried, let us bury her deeds with her.

Cheltenham starts tomorrow and most punters will go to the festival, at home. Thousands take holiday time or half-days or dodge.

27

Cheltenham Is No Place For Those With Corns Or Claustrophobics

March 11, 2013

L ADS will put on their best suits and head for town. Pretend for a while they really are at Cheltenham. It's a ritual. A few beers. Watch the racing in the pubs. Dart across to the betting shop, as they dodge the mad driving of boys with spots, in a hurry for the 2.30. The story is replicated all over Ireland. Cheltenham starts tomorrow and most punters will go to the festival, at home. Thousands take holiday time or half-days or dodge.

I like the betting shop. Soft seats. Warm. Pretty girls behind the counter. Free tea and biscuits. Debates on the racing. Ten screens showing every sport. The Chinese chattering away. Speaking even more quickly than the locals. An eastern Gaeltacht. All-day company for the racing lovers, the broke, the lonely, the bored, the talkers and the buzz-seekers. There would be a revolution in this country, if it were not for the betting shops.

There are laughs too. A portly man was asked by the shop stirrer how it was he was able to "even walk around with that big huge belly". Well, replied the large man, "Sure, I could hardly leave it at home." You have to be thick-skinned and clever to survive the raw, quick-draw repartee.

We are being turned upside down so as to make the money fall out of our pockets. But betting is fun and so are the shops. In moderation, like drinking. I was told another story in Browne's excellent betting shop in Listowel.

Canny track bookie Spike Murphy lays the dogs in Limerick and the horse in Cheltenham. Times are tough, even for bookies. Last week, two young lads were watching the satellite racing channels in Spike's house over in Abbeyfeale. Spike was out and about. The boys put down a three-briquette fire. The bookie was shocked at the waste. He took two briquettes off the grate. "Are ye trying to burn the house down", he said. You'll never beat the bookies, or Spike.

Every Cheltenham race is a championship and the atmosphere at the track would revive a man who fell asleep watching Dail Report. But Cheltenham is expensive. The entrance fee on Gold Cup day on The Club Enclosure is £80.

On Gold Cup Day the great grandchildren of the Black and Tans come to the track from the big cities. Loud they are and drunk too. There are fights, urinating in public and vomiting.

Cheltenham is full of pickpockets. Watch out. One busty woman I know keeps her money in her bra. God bless her. She has enough room in there for even Michael O'Leary's stash, but the men are always caught out. There's a lot to be said for loading up the underpants with your money. But even that's not safe. One of Cheltenham's poshest hotels hosts more hookers per square metre than any bar in Bangkok. The town centre pubs are packed after racing and it's a bit rough at times.

I wouldn't put you off going but Cheltenham is no place for gentility or those who suffer from claustrophobia and corns or addiction.

I have seen sane men who might only risk a tenner at home place a thousand on a horse at Cheltenham. Gambling is worse than drink in some ways. With the sauce it usually takes months before you go broke and ruin your health. There's a chance of intervention before too much damage is done but one bet written out on a docket in seconds can ruin families.

But Cheltenham for all its faults is a place to visit before you die.

Istabraq won for Ireland on my first year and the English threw their hats in the air. I remember thinking there couldn't have been any better place to be at that very moment, anywhere.

There's this long steep unforgiving hill at Cheltenham and when the drive comes on flaws will be found in horse or man. The crowd cheer for as many as 20 teams. There's no place to hide. No short cuts. Only the classiest, cleverest, fittest and most courageous win.

It was 1986 and Dawn Run's backers were tearing up their dockets into abstract origami. "The mare is beat," they cried.

John Joe O'Neill somehow lifted her over the last. It was as if he was carrying the mare. She reciprocated, galloped, possessed, relentlessly eating up every inch. The mare got up on the line to win the most thrilling Gold Cup ever run. Dawn Run was Irish, John Joe was Irish, owner Chairman Hill was Irish and trainer Paddy Mullins was Irish. No other country could have won that race. There were centuries of teaching and breeding timelined into the winning of it.

But I'm happy enough to stay put at home. You see a lot more on the television. The thronged betting shop throbs.

Happy enough sums it for most of us but in our hearts we know there's nowhere better than being there to witness the drama of it all. Nowhere better.

*I have a close friend who
was involved in the IRA.
He too has forsaken violence.
My friend is a good
and decent man.*

28

McGuinness Certainly Made The Most Of Life's Rare Second Chance

March 25, 2017

THE words redemption and forgiveness come straight from the lexicon of the Catholic Church. So do we forgive all sins, or none, or some? The first part of the Catholic process of forgiveness is sorrow and the second part is to make amends.

I met up with Martin McGuinness in The White House around this time last year. He was as courteous as could be. I told him how much we all owed him as a people. We had a couple of chats during the day. He was a people person and warm too. I was one of the first from the non-violent brigade to acknowledge his work on behalf of the peace process, in a sports column of all places, and he read it.

But somewhere in the back of my mind there at the steps leading up to the St Patrick's Day party was the near certainty that in his role as head of the IRA in Derry Mr McGuinness gave the orders. The case that comes to mind most is the murder of 29-year-old Joanne Mathers, who was killed in Derry because she was collecting census forms. The IRA was an equal opportunity killer. Jean McConville was murdered in Belfast for another insignificant "crime against the people". I think it is important the victims who died in the war are not forgotten or are seen as sacrificial footnotes to a peace process.

Mr McGuinness may have been responsible for violent deeds but he saved us all from another generation of violence. His motives were always the betterment of his people and the freedom of his country. Even his enemies cannot deny that much.

I have a close friend who was involved in the IRA. He too has forsaken violence. My friend is a good and decent man. But he explained "you would have to be there to know what it was like to be a Catholic living in the North. It was us or them after the British politicians gave the North over to the generals who were murdering b******s. There was a seething anger in all of us and we were all damaged from the savagery of a sectarian state".

I can understand the taking up of arms to defend one's community, but did the IRA go too far? "Yes" is his reply.

Mr McGuinness grew up in a country that didn't even allow the basic right of one man one vote. He failed his exams as a kid even though he had a brilliant mind because the plan was to keep the nationalists backward. These were crimes against children. Catholics were barricaded up in ghettos. Our brothers and sisters lived and died there in bondage. There is little doubt we in the south could have done more to help. In so many ways we backed our own people in to a corner and they had to fight their way out.

Maybe Martin should have chosen the peaceful road taken by John Hume and Mary McAleese. And he did, eventually. But Bloody Sunday, just around the corner from the McGuinness home, was a slaughter of the innocents. And there were lies and cover-ups. It was hard not to take up arms. Martin had the courage of his convictions and the convictions of his courage.

So how then did Mr McGuinness forsake violence? Here's my theory.

I have this vague memory of Babies Class in Listowel National School. This priest came in to tell us about sins. He told us we would go to hell and that it was very hot there. I'm pretty certain the priest ended up in hell himself as he was a paedophile. But that is a story for another day.

Our teacher Mrs Scanlan was a sound woman. She told us about the fire escape of confession and I still remember the relief. So even though I haven't been to confession for more than 30 years that sense of seeking forgiveness and making amends is very much ingrained in our Catholic psyche.

You can take the boy out of the Church but you can't take the Catholic out of the boy.

Confession as a concept is beautiful, in that there is forgiveness. There is also an admission of guilt. I'm not sure if Martin went far enough in asking for forgiveness but I think it is fair to say he went as far as he could, given the repercussions for him personally and the peace process in general. Mr McGuinness certainly made amends. He put his life on the line when he was fighting and he put his life on the line when he was at peace.

I'm not sure either of where he stood when it came to his position as regards the Church as an entity. Like most of us, he seemed to have had time for his local priests, who unlike their bosses in Rome put humanity before cant and dogma.

The whole idea of giving people a second chance seems to have fallen into disuse. The fact that Mr McGuinness was given the chance to change by people who believed in him like Bill Clinton, Bertie Aherne and Ms McAleese led to the miracle of peace in our beloved North.

The story of Martin McGuinness is indeed a Christian morality play. Too often we are too quick to condemn and it seems to me if a man or a woman makes a mistake well then he or she is permanently marked as tainted in the minds of those who define us by a single or series of unfortunate events. To forgive one must believe in the essential good in all of us. It may seem to you as a contradiction to describe this life-long republican as noble, but that's what he was. So what's it to be? Heaven or hell?

I have no doubt that the bellboy will hold the ascension door open for Mr McGuinness as he presses the button for the top floor.

Rugby Must Take Stand And Ban Unrepentant Vunipola From Final

April 22, 2019

BILLY VUNIPOLA is a homophobe. Vunipola is one of the best rugby players in the world. He is an England international who is key to his adopted country's World Cup hopes. Vunipola was awarded man of the match when his club Saracens defeated Munster in Coventry on Saturday in the semi-final of the Heineken Champions Cup.

Israel Folau, the Australian full-back, tweeted that "hell awaits" for "drunks, homosexuals, adulterers, liars, fornicators, thieves, atheists, idolators."

Vunipola backed Folau and refused to retract. So it was then that two of the best rugby players in the world agree with the burning of gay people in hell because they are gay. Yes burning, because that's what happens in hell.

Some of you who will say Vunipola is entitled to freedom of speech. More will profoundly disagree with the homophobic comments but maintain this is the man's religion and we are entitled to worship the God of our choice

There are religions whose followers kill non-believers. Religion must not be used a blanket defence.

Vunipola is a public figure who may not support the

punishment of gay people in this life but has no problem with punishment in the hereafter.

Vunipola is an influencer. His words will be heeded and acted upon for such is the nature of the world we live in. The cult of celebrity attracts the support of those who are extreme. One slur borrows another.

Nigel Owens is a gay rugby referee. Most would agree he too is world-class at what he does. His comments received massive support from rugby people.

Here's what Nigel Owens said: "Just judge a person on the decent person that they are. There are some things in life that you can choose — your sexuality is not one of them.

"I don't agree with the (Vunipola) opinion. Although everyone has the right to have his view, you then have to understand the consequences when you express the view that can be very, very hurtful to a lot of people.

"When people do cross that line of what is acceptable and what is not — particularly within the position of influence — then you have to take responsibility, I believe, for your actions."

Australia manager Michael Cheika fired Folau and rightly so, but Mark McCall, the Saracens coach, picked Vunipola to play against Munster. BT Sport awarded the man of the match award to Vunipola. They said "he had a hard week."

I'll tell you who had a hard week. It was the gay kids who are playing the game of rugby and will, according to Vunipola, burn in hell. And remember Nigel Owens tried to take his own life when he was a young man because of the shame he then felt.

Billy had more support from the fezzed Saracens fans who marched behind a band just in front of the entrance to the stand. They were late and missed the team bus.

The turn-out wasn't much more than the numbers of mourners walking behind the hearse carrying a reasonably popular man to an Irish country graveyard. They mixed freely with Munster. Songs were sung, drinks were drank and fun was had on a lovely sunny day.

Billy Vunipola snuck in to the Ricoh Arena, head down, through the human tunnel of hundreds of Munster fans. There was no fencing and scarcely any security. I thought I might have heard a few boos, but it was no more than the lowing of a stray sheep on a lonesome mountain.

There was a huge Saracens cheer though when Billy Vunipola's name was called out just before kick-off.

The cheer angered me and the Munster fans I spoke to felt the same. I felt so sorry for any gay person in the stadium or watching on TV.

Cheered

The total number of Saracens fans who were present was probably in the region of about 3,000. Not all cheered Vunipola.

The attendance was over 16,000 so I would say to the gay rugby community, the vast majority of us rugby supporters love you, and respect you for who you are. You are one of us and we are one of you.

To the kids, I would say, play on and enjoy the game. You will face bigotry, hate and ignorance wherever you go in life but you have nothing ever to be ashamed of. Wear the gay jersey and wear it with pride.

I'm pretty sure most of the Saracens supporters are not homophobic but their cheering of a homophobe was at best naïve and at worst an endorsement of Vunipola's beliefs.

The misguided cheers of the Saracens fans incensed a section of the Munster supporters on the far side from our position in the press box. Vunipola was booed. He stared into the crowd and a few boos turned to hundreds. Normally I would not condone booing but Munster are an inclusive club. No man or woman is left behind. Munster were expressing their support for our gay brothers and sisters.

Vunipola taunted the Munster fans after the game. There was no humility or sportsmanship here and a foolish person wearing a Munster jersey ran on to the pitch. This was no physical attack on the giant Vunipola. The incursion was a one-man invasion from a force of about 10,000 fans. The incursion must be condemned.

I wonder how Vunipola would feel if a fellow player said a person of colour would burn in hell because his skin was not white. The targeting of coloured players is bigotry of the worst kind and sport is fighting it every step of the way. Homophobia is an attack against the LGBT community, yet Vunipola was allowed to play against Munster on Easter Saturday.

Vunipola was warned by Saracens as to his future conduct. But after the game Vunipola said of Saracens: "Behind closed doors I was shown a lot of love."

Vunipola has had talks with the English RFU. England will not win the World Cup if he is fired. Vunipola has since declared: "I believe in what I believe in. There was no intention to hurt anyone."

Well Billy, flames do tend to hurt people. And kids do look up to big name players. You have hurt so many people.

Rugby must take a stand. Billy Vunipola must be banned from playing in next month's Heineken Champions Cup Final.

30

Honest, Fearless, Loyal And Funny — For Foley It Was Never About 'Me', Always About The Team

October 17, 2016

ANTHONY FOLEY wore his heart like a crest on his Munster shirt and in the end the heart that beat so strong in the heat of battle gave out on him.

Munster mourns and Ireland weeps. 'Too young' and 'too soon' are the words we speak. He was the kind of man we felt would shoulder the old guard's caskets. He was the keeper of the flame and the keeper of the faith.

The heart that sustained us all and gave us identity and unity beats no more. All of our hearts are broken. But that was the public man.

He was a dad too and a son and a brother and a husband. I know his family. They are the kindest and the nicest. The shock must have been truly awful.

His dad Brendan was there in Paris to hold his boy in his arms. That much we can be thankful for. And how proud he was of his son who carried on the tradition with Shannon, Munster and Ireland.

The Foleys are an emotional, loving family and I just can't get the image of the dad and son out of my head. Brendan would gladly have swapped places.

Yes, his dad can be proud. His son was honest, fearless, loyal and funny.

Like the rest of us, he had his moments of self-doubt. The job as Munster head coach was demanding and at times the criticism was unrelenting. It couldn't be good for you. But Anthony didn't throw a fit of pique when he was asked to share the coaching role last summer. For Foley, it was never about the 'me', but all about the 'us'.

Munster, Shannon and Ireland were his passion but his wife Olive and their two boys were his life. He was a family man first. He adored his wife and his sons. He really did and this just isn't the usual obituary blather. Olive is lovely and she sings. I was there when we were beaten and she lifted her man with her words and smiles and laughs.

We were good old pals. I always stuck up for him because I had great faith in him as a man and as a coach. I hugged his sweaty jersey in the press conference when we won the Heineken Cup for the first time in 2006. I broke all the rules. Foley was the captain. "Hey," he said, "I'll bet you're dying to write about that. Don't forget to spell my name right."

I used to call him The Holy of Foleys and he was just that for all of us who followed him.

I'm watching the TV now. The Munster fans are singing 'The Fields of Athenry' outside the Stade Colombes where Munster were supposed to be playing. Lonely lie the fields around Thomond Park. We are good to each other when it matters most.

Foley was the link between the strands that make up Munster rugby. His dad beat the All Blacks in 1978. Anthony played when rugby was amateur and then he was a pro when we were the champions of Europe in 2006. The bond firmed and followed on when he was made assistant coach and then head coach. His story is the story of Munster. Foley captained his country and played for Ireland more than 60 times.

They are just showing our hero now on TV, back in 2006 when he was our captain in Cardiff. His little boy is in his arms. So happy he is there out on the pitch with 80,000 of us singing our hearts out. But this time 'The Fields' is not a Paris lament but a Cardiff te deum.

We won at last. And Foley is babysitting. That was him all over. Family first.

I'm thinking back to a chat we had many years ago. It was all about self-deprecation with Foley. It was his way of maintaining his modest demeanour, which is a huge part of the Munster psyche. Big heads are shrunk more often in the Munster dressing room than by blowpipers in the Amazon back waters.

I asked: "Foley, how come you seem to run faster than the lads you are playing against, even though they are faster than you?"

"I start before them" was his answer.

And it was true. He always made the right decisions on the pitch. Up he'd peep from the back of the scrum and then when he could see the space, off he'd go. He was over the line even before the opposition sentinels raised the alarm.

"If Napoleon had Foley as a general, they'd be speaking French in Moscow" are words I wrote.

"Will you stop," he said.

Jonathan Sexton told me of Foley's lines to the Irish team when he was defence coach under Declan Kidney. The call was 'a warrior is brought off the field on his shield'. He was very nice to a young Leinster kid back then.

Foley was respected and admired all over the rugby world.

There's a text from Keith Wood, his team mate, close friend and near neighbour.

I told Woody I could hardly see the laptop with the tears.

"I can't stop crying myself," was his reply.

Mick Galwey, or Gaillimh as Munster people call him, is in a bad way.

Anthony was in Kilkenny last weekend for Gaillimh's fiftieth. I'm thinking now of Bob Dylan's line: "When she cries, she cries just like a little girl". These two tough, big men, Gaillimh and Woody, are crying like small boys for their lost friend.

Gaillimh can barely talk in between the gulps. "Last week we were having a pint together and he was telling me if I was playing nowadays I'd be too small for mascot."

He pauses for air. "Axel (his nickname) took over from me as captain of Munster and do you know even though I knew I was finished and was sad over that, the relief was there that the right man had the honour now. I was so delighted when I saw Axel walking in the door to the party. At least he met his friends for one last farewell."

Anthony stayed with my brother John for Mick's party. He lost some of that camaraderie when he became coach. Now he was with his old comrades and loving every minute of it all. Foley was never fitter. "No one could have suspected he had heart trouble," says John.

Above all else, we always felt safe in his company. That man would never do an ugly thing and there was something in his eyes that read you through to the core. He would sense if your form was bad and he would tailor his conversation from ribbing to empathy. The humanity in him would try to lift you.

He was a minder and a safe-keeper of bodies and souls, of traditions and of values. And his family will be safe too. Anthony Foley will never leave Olive and his boys. This powerful, eternal love will last forever. The Holy of Foleys will always look out for his loved ones.

For Anthony Foley never let the side down.

It's the annual homecoming for the Listowel Races. I love these first few days. Lads I was at school with drop in.

31

Listowel Races, The People's Meeting, Where The Best Of Times Are Guaranteed

September 10, 2018

IT is Saturday — the night before the race. Ellie Mac was the first one to bed. She lay down in her stable by the River Feale and slept to the soothing sounds of water flowing over stone.

The neighbours had been coming home all week. From Australia mostly, and a good few of the older lads from America landed down the road in Shannon. Then our people returned from England over the weekend.

It's the annual homecoming for the Listowel Races. I love these first few days. Lads I was at school with drop in. Within seconds it's as if we were still back in St Mike's. Like as if they never left. But they did. In their thousands.

I'm upstairs now over the pub looking out at Market Street.

The Moriartys put up the rows of shiny lights. And the primary colours are bobbing in the breezes. Sean Moriarty passes by.

I shout out the window: "Hey Sean, the fourteenth light on the ninth row is gone out."

For a second he looks around and then he knows and walks away home for the supper.

Behind him in the old cattle market Bird's Amusement's big dipper digs its beak like a Texan oil well. I can nearly hear the screams from our front window. Birds are our Disneyland, our Las Vegas and I'll be bringing my little niece Lily over to The Market. She's eight and I wonder if she will still love the merry-go-rounds or has she gone too big for them now.

I put on the fire. The hard, dry black turf lights up the room into life. The cousins will be staying over. I think then of Sean Moriarty's rules. Sean would never see anyone stuck for a bed and he never charges. It's part of the tradition here to look after the visitors. Sean's three terms and conditions for his guests are strict. "No smoking, no breakfast and no sex."

I get word the Ellie Macs have arrived. Ellie Mac runs tomorrow in the Cheesestrings Novice Chase. She's owned by the Niccolai Schuster Racing syndicate, made up of Nicc's school pals from St Mary's and his family. Nicc died when the balcony collapsed in Berkeley. He loved the races. My Aunty, Peg Keane, was his grandmother.

Ellie needs good ground so I put out The Infant De Prague — a holy statue used to ward off rain. Nicc's pals tell me they are just back from Prague and they saw the Infant in person. Surely a sign and there was another. Nicc's Granddad John lived in Prague. The rain stops.

But Ellie is up against it. Willie Mullins has three in the race. Ellie is 14/1 but soon the odds will tumble.

Race Day Sunday.

The Infant only works shift. It's raining again. I dress up in blue of St Marys and the red of Bayern Munich, Nicc's teams.

Listowel is the people's meeting and the harvest festival. The turf, hay and silage are home now. In the hurling lands, the corn is safely stored in the giant silos. Old friends return and we take a roll call of those who have departed.

I'm sad for my dad who loved the Listowel Races. Dad would be practising his songs for weeks before. He sang while shaving.

Buzzed

Ellie is buzzed before the race. All the Cahersiveen O'Connor cousins are here, along with Nicc's dad John and his mom Graziella. John and Graz keep the spirits up. The last time we were all together was at the funeral of our uncle Denis just a few months ago.

Ellie is going off her head but that's when she's at her best.

We meet Henry de Bromhead, one of the greatest trainers there is. He tells us the ground is dead. Ellie needs it faster but she's fit and big for a mare. Ellie tries to break free. She rears, kicks and bucks.

They go off at a furious pace and Ellie jumps very well. The Paul Townend-ridden Camelia de Cotte is the hot favourite and she looks all over a winner coming in to the straight. But Ellie stays and stays. The fans are going crazy. Go on Ellie. Please, please. But try as she might and brilliant as Rachel Blackmore rode, the winning post came too soon. And Paul Townend rode a perfect race.

The syndicate cheered as if Ellie had won the Grand National. For John and Graz, it was all about putting on a show on home ground. All about a coming together on a happy occasion. All about sportsmanship and the taking part.

Henry de Bromhead was pleased. "We might come back here next year for The Guinness Kerry National," he says. "Ellie stays and stays. The longer the better."

Rachel Blackmore was happy. "She jumped really well

but she hit the third-last." The non-whingers syndicate thank Rachel. She's smothered in hugs.

"I'll bet that's the first time you ever got such a welcome when you finished second," says Henry.

I was on my way over the bridge to back home when the prices were called out. Ellie was backed from 14s in to 4s but there was no big bets. This was fivers and twos and one-euro bets by the locals and the whole of St Mary's. Our friends wanted to share in the memory of Nicc, who was a joy and full of his fun.

It was some communal punt.

As I was leaving the course I meet Liam Sheahan, whose cousin Aoife Beary was seriously injured in the Berkeley tragedy. When I was a boy the horses were led from the Dublin train in to Aoife's ancestral pub, just up from John B's. Aoife's dad Mickey, a fine fellow, is also from Listowel.

Aoife Beary spoke to the Californian senate and swung the vote to force builders who have had negligence claims to declare same. Thanks to Aoife's bravery, as well as her eloquence, lives will be saved.

Too late for Nicc and the five more who died, but there is life after death when we remember those we love in the places they would love to be.

I'm off to pull pints for a week and I'll be telling stories of how John, Graz and Alexi — Nicc's younger brother — are trying to come to terms with their grief. The family and friends unite behind the common cause of having fun with Ellie, the people's mare, here at the people's racecourse, in the town their Nicc loved so well.

32

Farewell Mike Lawlee, The Local Character Who Loved To Help Others

February 19, 2018

THE street-scape changes forever when a small-town street man dies. I see him now rushing from his van — the one with the road visible under the floor, and the sliding door that wouldn't slide.

The van is left abandoned with the engine running on a double yellow. Mike Lawlee is in a mad hurry to lay off a bet for Browne Bookmakers in Paddy Power before the price is gone.

Mike is togged out in just-below-the-knee shorts, and his varicose veins are purple slugs. He wears a straw hat like a cowboy would wear on his day off, and his shorts would fall down without the wide-as-a-motorway multi-coloured braces.

The white tennis socks are worn inside the sandals and his glasses are hanging off him like a necklace in case he forgets them in the bookies.

The sandals flip-flop-flap faster and the tempo increases. Lawlee only looks out in front, like a soldier going over the top. He rushes into the betting shop. Man on a mission, and it was top secret. No leaks here. The bet was down. Just in time.

We lost Mike last week. He was part of our town, part

of us, one of our own, part of our growing up and part of our winding down, a man made by us and himself, but a man who will never be made again. He was what is known as a character.

Everyone loved Mike. He was the man who couldn't say no to a request for help. Lawlee had a heart of gold but his heart was only working at 20pc. The heart that helped so many killed him in the end. His brother and four sisters were all around him when he was jumping the last. He loved each and every one of them and they loved him. He was only 65.

When my poor old dad was on the way out himself, his death bed was very uncomfortable. Mike made four trips to Tralee for a hospital bed, but every time there was some bit missing or broken or didn't fit. There were times when Mike's execution didn't quite match his resolve. My dad said: "I'll be dead and buried before Lawlee comes back with the bed."

But back he came, on the hottest day for years. Lawlee was dripping with the sweat. And Dad slept sound. He loved Lawlee. They were neighbours. Dad 'got' Lawlee.

Once, I was due in France to write about a Munster match but I got excited and drank too much the night before. So I call Lawlee at 4am and ask him to drive me to Shannon. I slept all the way to the airport. "We're here" said Lawlee. It was Kerry Airport.

"Is there a boat?" he asked. I still made the game in time.

Mike was a penciller for Browne Bookmakers back before laptops. He had a phenomenal head for figures. I see him again at Galway Races. The bets are flying in. It's as hot as hell. Eric Browne shouts the odds out to Lawlee. This is make or break for the year but Mike never makes a mistake. His brain was wired for maths.

I look down. Lawlee's feet are planted in a basin of water. Eric's border collie Butch is drinking from another basin. There's a crush to rush to back at Browne's better odds. Lawlee asks me if I know anyone who has a barber's chair for a man looking for one. Eric threatens him with instant death.

The story of the mattresses sums Mike up. Lawlee traded in second-hand goods such as cookers. He even sold an old floral pee pot as a flower pot. Mike was often given the job of clearing out the houses of the deceased. Sad now isn't it? His own house is next up. It will be some job. The unsold uncollectibles are piled high as the ceiling.

There is no great sale for second-hand mattresses. And the local council warned Mike that burning was illegal, on a number of occasions. The mattresses were piled as high as a house in Browne's yard and a neighbour suggested, jokingly, that Mike should bring them to Ballybunion Golf Club where they could be used as coastal protection from the pounding of the Atlantic.

Mike duly arrived at the prestigious golf club with a van full of mattresses but his gracious offer was declined in a very abrupt fashion.

Lawlee once drove me to Cork for a colonoscopy as there's a sedative involved. Dr Billy Stack comes in behind the screen with the picture of my colon. "Do you see the redness there?" says Dr Billy pointing to the lit up shot of darkest me.

"I do Dr Billy. You better fix that up," says Lawlee, who had snuck in behind the screen unbeknownst to us.

That was Lawlee. He never worried about himself. He only ever worried about us.

Lawlee was just so generous, and he brought presents to kids. He would empty his pockets for a good cause, and I mean empty. Mike never charged a poor person for the use of the van.

We are all distraught. The only way to cope is by telling the stories, as if in some way the recall is keeping him alive.

I should be walking down town soon to check to see if the pub is still there. Sunday was his day for a few pints and a few bets. I'm not sure if I can face the street today.

Mike was very close to bookmaker Berkie Browne and his wife Kelly. It was Berkie who told me the sad news.

"He's a saint now Berkie," I said. And Berkie, with tears in his eyes, replied: "He was a saint when he was alive."

33

The Pitch Invader Against Kerry, Fancy Dress To Beat Croker Ban And Spooky Story That Will Have Mayo Fans Dreaming

August 14, 2017

THERE are no lamentations out of Big Mick Barrett, the man who jumped the Walls of Limerick.

The word lamentation brings with it the picture of an old hag wailing above the screeching wind and pouring rain on a wild Atlantic headland far away from faraway places in old Mayo of the perpetual sorrow.

But this image of Mayo couldn't be further from the truth. Mayo people are endlessly optimistic. The great deeds of the Mayo team are a glorious ode to the ethos of always giving your all and never giving up.

"Will ye beat Kerry, Mick?

"Of course we will win. Why wouldn't we?"

And, who you might ask, is Big Mick Barrett?

Mick is the man who invaded the field of play when his beloved Mayo met Kerry in the Gaelic Grounds some three years ago in that epic semi-final replay when Kerry won in extra-time. Mick didn't really invade the pitch. It was more of case of the pitch invading him.

Mick couldn't help himself. He was taken over by the red and green mist.

Anyone of us, and I wouldn't be great myself, who are inclined to get excited at games felt for Mick, even if he did cross the line. I know he shouldn't have run out onto the field and he was suspended for a year. But there was no one killed and no one was going to be killed.

"What came over you at all?" I ask Mick.

"Sure there was a melly (melee) and we were being bate all over the place. And one of our lads got sent off in the melly or whatever it is you call it. Before I knew it I was on the pitch."

"And what would you have done to the ref, Mick?"

"Ah sure nottin. I was only going to say something to him."

And now three years on Mick says he hadn't a clue exactly what he was going to say to the ref only that "it wouldn't be good but I wouldn't use any bad language or anything".

I didn't have the heart to tell Mick his tilt at the windmill sent him in the direction of the linesman. Mick couldn't see the wood for the trees.

Mick's daughter Laura was the heroine of the piece. She ran out after Mick and tried to stop him, but Laura might as well have thrown herself in front of a bulldozer freewheeling down Croagh Patrick for all the hope she had of halting her dad's bull run.

Laura was only 17 at the time. It took some courage and some love for her dad to do what she did in front of 50,000 people. The teenager was the victim of vile internet abuse.

"That wasn't right," said Mick with some sadness in his voice. "That wasn't right at all. I'm fair game. It wasn't Laura's fault at all. She was very upset."

I think it was the father-daughter part that got me interested in Mick's story.

I go to most of the games with my daughter Lainey who was a handy enough player. She keeps me from going over the edge. And there are times when I need fencing in.

"She's a super girl," says Mick. "I'm always No 1 with Laura."

"Did the missus give out to you, Mick?"

"Oh sure she did. I'm still in the black books." Mick's wife Marie is from Louisburgh.

She's the greatest woman in the world," says Mick. His young lad has no interest in football and Mick observes: "And would you blame him after seeing me in action?"

That giving-out from Laura and Marie was a worse penalty than the suspension. Sources close to Mick, the source might even be Mick himself, tell of how the suspended man was seen wearing a maroon wig in Croke Park.

"Did you dress up as a woman, Mick?"

"Ah no," he laughs, "I wouldn't be good looking enough."

Mick and Marie worked hard in England. The young couple came home to Mayo about 15 years ago with their kids.

Mick is a small builder. There's a hint of the bad times in his voice when he says, "Work is nothin' hectic at the moment. But things are picking up. Ireland is the best country in the world. I couldn't wait to come home when I was over across the water."

I wouldn't be standing up for Mick if he was a blackguard. I had him well checked before I wrote this piece. Mick is very well got in Mayo.

He asks if I have a spare ticket. We will do our best. But Mick, your ticket will be so near the roof of Croke

Park, you'll need to abseil down the Hogan to get on to the field.

Mick will be travelling to Dublin with his three body-guards — Colm MacMenamin, Michael Cooney and John Joe Chambers.

"We won't be staying in Dublin but we will stay over for the final.

"Ah but we had some craic at last year's final. We went up in one of them, what do you call 'em? Like a bike pulling a wheelbarrow."

"Is it rickshaws, Mick?"

"That's it, rickshaws."

Then he tells the story of the new doctor.

"I do a bit of business with this lad and his wife told me she went to a fortune teller before the birth of her child about 27 years ago. The fortune teller told her the child would be a girl and that she would become a doctor. But wait till I tell you. She told her that when the child would get her first pay cheque, Mayo would win the All-Ireland."

And you all know what's coming next. Says Mick, with glee: "You'd never guess, but didn't the daughter, the doctor, get her first pay cheque only the other day. Sure doesn't that bate any stupid curse about funerals. Ye are gone, ye are gone, Billy. Come on Meeo!"

Lads will ye spancel that man next Sunday.

I will never change my colours but good luck to you Mick Barrett. And Mick, for feck sake, this time, will you try your best to stay behind the white line.

34

Some Of Us Were Not Made To Sit On Horses High Up Over The Battlefield

March 22, 2014

THE watching of the match is a pure pleasure now. Like sinking into a hot bath after a hard day. Then you rewind the TV to watch the best bits again. It's the very same as turning on the hot tap for a refill, with your curled-in toes. The ease and the stress-free surge renews and restores. Wordsworth describes the experience as 'emotion recollected in tranquillity.'

We've already written about the game, but like the Christmas turkey, there's enough meat left to knock the second day out of it. The most common remark from the Irish we met after the Six Nations grand finale was that "you couldn't enjoy it." Strange that. But true. The tension was gnawing away at nerve endings like the off-piste Japanese rat that plunged the infamous Fukushima nuclear plant near Tokyo into darkness around this time last year.

The mayor of Paris gave us free train rides to make up for the high levels of air pollution in the city. Just to breathe was impossible in that last, few minutes, but the gasoline fumed air wasn't the cause of our discomfort. It was the match that never rested. The match that stole our breath away.

I have a hazy recollection of a movie where this distressed woman went into a panic attack in a train hijack, or then again it could have been a runaway train. Either way there was a loss of control. Like the mad match, you were taken on a crazy journey with no stops until the end.

The man sitting next to the hysterical lady took his bagel out of a brown paper bag. The usual Holywood cure for hysterical people in the movies was a slap across the face, but the man who was sitting next to the screaming lady made her breathe in and out of the brown-paper bagel bag. The hysterical lady was in great old form after the intervention by the kindly man until he was shot by a hijacker, presumably for not minding his own business.

But nobody near me had a brown bag. Then the heart started pounding. I was going to ask someone to wallop me across the face.

I had no travel insurance. Ryanair charged a fortune for the flight and there was no way I was giving them any more. That would make it three iconic Irish writers who died in Paris – me, Jimmy Joyce and Oscar Wilde.

The terrible recall, the awful déjà vu of the All Blacks' last play try was waiting to happen all over again. There was a sense of inevitability. The feeling that we in Ireland were life's victims.

Or maybe we were eternally cursed because a foolhardy Irish tourist gave his girlfriend a French kiss up against the slanty wall of Tutankhamen's isosceles tomb. We should have been more detached, us old pros, but it couldn't be done. Some of us were never made to sit on horses, high up over the battlefield.

When Jonathan Sexton was stretchered off, we feared the worst. He's much better now. We did our own check up. "Where's the Eiffel Tower?" we asked him on Monday night? He got that one. Jonathan gave us some fright. Rugby is a dangerous game.

Sexton scored two great tries and nailed that second half pressure penalty to win the Six Nations, but if we had lost he would have shipped a share of blame due to the two missed kicks in the first half. But he was saved by the intervention of three of his less experienced team-mates. "Merci," he said to them. The French is getting better every day.

Only now in the calm after the storm can a proper report be written of the game's last plays.

The French were singing La Marseillaise, as if they had already won. Up the field they swept. Exhausted Ireland were outnumbered and outflanked. The clock was ticking away faster than our hearts.

Dave Kearney took a massive gamble. The French looked certain to score in the corner. All they had to do was transfer the ball efficiently, but out bolted Kearney who left his wing to get to the giant second-row Pascal Pape.

Kearney didn't quite nail Pape before he got the ball away, but he did enough to ensure the final pass dribbled forward. The wait for the TV ref's call was excruciating. Most of the French in our stand thought it was a try.

This French man in a purple trousers celebrated by kissing his young son who was also wearing purple trousers. They're mad for the purple pants in France.

The RTE viewing figures will be given at around a million, but the real numbers for that last play will be just five. The famous five; with hearts and lungs as sound as a smith's bellows.

The rest of Ireland were out in the garden, or in a toilet, or under a hedge, or hugging each other for comfort, unable to watch, praying like mad, and breaking into old jars of left-over valium from the time the oul fellah had the bad back or the mother had the change or ransacking drawers for brown paper bags.

The try was disallowed. Scrum for Ireland. Dave I hope you still have the programme we gave you at the back of the posts where ROG scored his famous drop-goal to win the Grand Slam in 2009. Now you have two winning programmes. And Dave, you're in this one.

Back into the house with the one million. Ireland lose the scrum. The French have it. They're setting it up for the drop-goal.

Back out again go the million. The million pine for Brian. Will his last cap end in tragedy? The off-the-fags smokers are mummified in nicotine patches. An old lady told us she blamed herself for not replacing the red bulb that was supposed to light up The Sacred Heart.

The two relative rookies Devin Toner and Chris Henry saved the day. They grabbed the Frenchman carrying the ball and embraced him in a suffocating waltz. The rest of the pack back them up.

You could pack the Irish eight into a lunch box. They are all for one and one for all. Mr Walsh, the referee, gives the scrum to us and with a dramatic flourish he blows the final whistle. Ireland are the Six Nations champions.

Back in go the one million to the TV.

The French father and son in the purple pants stand to applaud both teams. So do the rest of the 80,000 in the ground. So do we all. Even now a week on, the encores are still being clapped in every part of our country and our collective unconfined joy has not diminished one bit.

35

Not Only Did He Want To Marry My Mother, But He Wanted To Take The Pub As His Dowry

May 12, 2014

THE old boy stood in front of our pub and pointed up at the mounted lettering.

"My name will be up there soon," he said.

The man was a suitor for the mother and he had no chance of success. I'll go further. He had no chance whatsoever.

Not only did he want to marry the mother but he wanted to take my pub as well as part of his due dowry. "Look," I said to him, "you can marry the mother but you'll have to sign a pre-nup."

He had a better chance of prising the queen away from Prince Philip. I was very much aware that customers are a valued commodity in the pub business right now but I couldn't help myself.

It could have been some sort of a variation of the Oedipus complex that broke out in me but there was no way I was going to call him Dad. There's this lady of indeterminate age whom we have often referred to here as "the woman who hasn't had sex in 37 years".

It seemed to me like a perfect fit but the randy suitor didn't bother with her. He had it very bad for the mother. She was somewhere around the 80 mark back then and the oul' lad was about six or seven years older.

So I got to thinking. And the question I was asking myself is, what age do men lose the mind for women? I put this one to a 90- something-year-old. "Ask me in 10 years time," was his defiant reply.

Then the mother was on TV twice in the past few weeks and a man from the midlands who never met her wants to marry her off the television. He proposed by letter and in the old-fashioned way. He asked me for my mother's hand.

I was going to write back that he could have her bad hip instead. The mother insisted, though, that he be treated with respect.

I turned him down for her with a polite but firm reply. What I would really have loved to write was will you ever feck off and stop trying to rob my mother off me. He put a bar of chocolate in with the marriage proposal letter. Fruit and nut. The mother refused to eat it in case it would be interpreted as giving him some sort of encouragement. Not that he would know. For the record I ate it for her, even though the mother instructed me to send it back.

I'll tell her the paper didn't come in this morning as the delivery lorry was punctured or the piece was spiked by the lawyers or a lover of literature, so don't go telling her now.

She'd probably find out anyway. My mother should have been a PI. She loves investigating things. The continuing investigation into the detection of the toilet paper thief has taken a new twist. There was a roll stolen from the gents on Saturday night. Up until now we thought the thief was a woman. Or at least we think the thief was a woman because the paper was stolen from the ladies. This is a serious development as we can hardly put CCTV cameras in the toilets.

Now she wants me to get involved in the investigation. As if it's not bad enough to have to be on the look- out for horny octogenarians showing off to the mother by riding bikes with no hands up and down the road outside the front of the pub and trying to seduce her by sending on bars of fruit and nut in the post.

I'm going to sue Viagra, Ciallis and any other tablet that makes old men young.

There was a great order in the world when men retired gracefully from the fray after years of service. It's like giving past-it footballers flying feet.

There's a man whose most earnest wish is to grow old gracefully and he told me lately he has no interest whatsoever in the other thing, which is what we call sex in Kerry.

Sometimes, some of the people who read this column ask me if all this stuff really happens. It does, it does. In fact there are occasions when I have to leave out true stories because the tales are beyond belief. I've lost track of the amount of people who have asked me if the woman who hasn't had sex for 37 years really exists.

The improbable and shocking story of the man who lost interest in sex is true.

I asked him if he might try out the Viagra. His heart, so far as we know, is in good nick and I couldn't see any harm in his putting up the bit of scaffolding, but he was a conscientious objector who would not interfere with the natural decline in sexual function.

"I'll take my baten," he said.

But then again, could you blame a man for wanting to extend his sex life well into the golden years? There might be a dividend, too, for his partner... or maybe it might be that she'd like a bit of rest.

An old man is as much entitled to a bit of the other thing as a young man.

I have no problem at all with the notion of eternal lovemaking. But stay away from my mother. She only ever loved the one man and even though he's no longer with us her fidelity endures.

36

'Ring' Cycle – A Day Out Like No Other And the Jewel In Kingdom's Crown

April 8, 2019

JIMMY DUFFY from Blennerville pedalled the famed Ring of Kerry charity cycle on an old-fashioned, throw-your-leg-over-the-bar bicycle.

Someone said the bike was so old it could have belonged to Michael Collins.

There was a basket on the front, a carrier on the back and a bell Jimmy never rang, for fear of offending anyone.

Jimmy togged out in Kerry football shorts, an unbuttoned-up white shirt, ordinary socks and his going-to-Mass shoes pedalled him up mountains. There was 'ere a sign of lycra. Jimmy cycled to the town of Killarney, where Ireland's biggest one-day charity cycle kicks off on July 6 this year.

The Ring of Kerry Cycle is to Kerry what JP McManus is to Limerick. The event has raised nearly €16 million to date and there isn't a place or a person who has not benefited.

Jimmy might drink a pint on the way around the mountains and lakes and seas that God designed on the last day of creation. By then your Almighty, and mine, would have had plenty of experience of making beautiful places.

The Ring of Kerry is God's masterpiece.

The mountains should be framed and hung in a gallery. The colour changes the shades of the contours depending on the vagaries of cloud and sun, with the taller mountains peeping out over the shoulders of the foothills, all to get a better look at the wild or kind Atlantic.

I had two aunts living in Cahersiveen, the town that hugs the mountain. Sadly, they have both passed on now. I remember the size of the South Kerry big skies when I was a boy. I still have that sense of wonder. And I feel tiny but at the same time elevated spiritually.

The scenes out over the seas are like nowhere else on earth and when you look from the cliffs of Iveragh to the spit of Inch in the middle, and the Dingle Peninsula beyond, the cares of today, tomorrow and yesteryear are put on hold or explained.

There's splendour here around every corner.

I think it may have been Stephen Roche who was asked if he enjoyed the scenery of the savage Tour de France mountain stage to Alpe d'Huez. "I was just watching the wheel of the riders in front of me," said Roche.

The Ring of Kerry Charity Cycle isn't a race but you can race if you like. There's freedom to do as you wish. Most of you will take time to stop for a while on the road to, or in Cahersiveen, Kenmare, Sneem, Derrynane, Glenbeigh and Puck.

The Ring got too big and there were 12,000 cyclists taking part. The organisers meant well. They were doing their best for the charities but truth to tell there were just too many cyclists on the narrow roads.

This year's cycle has been limited to 8,000. More than 1,500 volunteers will help with feeding stations, medics and the locals who continue the tradition of hospitality.

My cousin Bridget Maguire is chairperson of the steering committee. She reminds me so much of her Aunty Mary, my Mom. Straight, but caring, no fuss and no drama. She is one of many but our family are deadly proud of her.

You can be certain the cycle will be superbly organised. There are staggered starts and the fast bikers who want to get off first get a free run.

The organisers hope to bring back the cyclists who maybe felt they were held up by the crowds a few years back.

But most stop along the way and some of the riders take up to eight hours to complete the spin.

The scene at the finish in Killarney beats the Tour de France. There are bands and food, hugs, and lots of love. Friends and families are there to meet the cyclists.

This is fun but it's tough too. The cycle is 175 kilometres and if you want that in miles divide by eight and multiply by five. You can make it as tough or as easy as you like.

Don't forget to call to see Betty Breen of Kelly's Cross who paints her home a different colour every year and gives tea to all.

The big thing though is you will raise money for charity and maybe find figuring out in the beauty of Kerry. This is a voluntary event, run by the people, for the people.

I am an ambassador this year for the Kerry Rape and Sexual Abuse Centre, a place of great love where the professional counselling helps victims to find their way through the suffering. All of the named charities are worthy of our support.

This day has changed lives. The girl had a puncture near Sneem. The man stopped to help. They met up again at the finish in Killarney.

He gave her the engagement ring at the end of the Ring the following year. The committee surprised the happy couple with a guard of honour at their wedding in Fossa a year later. The bicycle wheels were formed in to an arch, in the same way hurlers toast the bride and groom with hurls.

Cathal Walsh, the friendliest PRO, who was on the first Ring with 34 others, told me that Jimmy, well in to his sixties, would cycle back to Blennerville via the Short Mountain.

The bike didn't have gears but Jimmy did. There was no empty light in the stamina tank.

The Short Mountain is a long old climb, but the hero always made sure to hydrate at The Shanty Bar in Bally-finnane.

It was a day out like no other and still is.

He's gone now is Jimmy, but the cycle he loved, for the people he loved, keeps on giving.

37

Heed My Purple Prose: We Don't Need Wall-To-Wall Cream

July 28, 2014

SO there I was lying in bed, in the middle of the night, with the weight of the world wearing down on top of me. I had to lie flat. The back is gone again. I started to worry, as you do late at night.

The news is the stuff of nightmares. For a good while it was all about the depression, or was it a recession? Now it's the Middle East again.

So I got to thinking, what could I do about it all anyway?

I took out the frustration out on the cream ceiling. I hate cream – the colour. It's not as if you could stand up on the bed and spoon some of the ceiling on top of a bowl of jelly or apple pie. Cream is Ireland's favourite colour. Put down the paper for a second or ignore the tablet. Take a look around you. I'll bet there's a cream something in every direction and not just in the middle of a bun.

I know a woman who daubs new cream over coats of old cream. Her house is about the half the width it used to be. If you stood still long enough the chances are she would deem you to be an inanimate object and would proceed to paint you cream. The lady even paints the radio cream.

Don't take any notice of me this week if I jump a little bit here and there. The back is gone again. The mother has steadfastly refused to lift any more barrels and so I had to hoist up a barrel of beer all on my own. I'd fire her but 59 years' redundancy would sink the ship. Now I'm doped up to the last.

One of the drugs is a generic version of valium, which was given to women in the old days by mostly male doctors to stop them giving out to the husbands.

But then the doctors discovered it was a muscle relaxant and men with bad backs, which is close on 100pc of us. The drugs are to combat spasms which are very similar to contractions women go through when they are having babies. When I was in the maternity ward the nurses used always say, "if men could have babies, there would be no children born".

This was of course a snide reference to the fiction that all men are softies who whinge at the slightest sign of any pain. The story we are sold is that if a man gets sick it's manflu and there's really nothing wrong with him. The worst ones though are the odd women who say, "ah you poor thing" in a really pitying and insincere voice, and you know what they really mean is men give in too easy and if there was a big match to go to the back would clear up almost immediately.

My theory is this approach has killed millions of us men. We could have two broken legs and the diagnosis from some women would be, sure, it's all psychosomatic. Note I wrote some, not all. The inference is there's nothing wrong with us and we shouldn't be bothering the doctors who are far too busy as it is consoling women whose husbands couldn't be bothered talking to them about their troubles. Most men only go to the doctor when it's far too late and the attitude that we have a low or no pain threshold plays a major role in this. So that was one of the worries that was brought on by the cream ceiling.

I would have welcomed a squashed moth or a dead fly just to break up the monotony of it all. What is this national obsession with insipid frigging cream? Why can't we paint our country in bright colours like red? I painted the front of the pub in the green and gold of Kerry and the red of Munster. Cream reminds me of cat's vomit and the pale faces of sick people.

The morning dose is kicking in now and I'm getting very drowsy. There's a note stuck on to the side of tablet bottle that says 'do not operate any heavy machinery' so I begin to wonder if that includes the TV zapper. I must remember not to drive my crane today.

The door of my old room over the pub is cream. I had to move down here to write because of the noise in my own house where a new shower is being installed because we are too clean a family and are always wearing out showers. The tiles around the shower are cream. I'm ready to go on a dirty protest.

There should be only so many cream buildings allowed in every town and city. Dublin City Council could lead the way, what with their excellent track record in banning things.

I swear it to you here and now: I will paint my old room purple the very minute I get the back sorted. As for the tiles, someone told me you can stick pictures of fishes and mermaids. I'm going to make up those paper blobs with spit on them and throw them hard up to the ceiling where they will stick for a stalactite effect.

The war on cream starts here.

Here's a warning now: if you are against words like penis and vagina, give up reading and don't be writing letters to my boss telling him I'm a pervert and there's no place in a family newspaper for penises and vaginas.

38

There's Nothing Wrong With Naked — But This Country Is Too Small And Too Cold For Nudity

May 26, 2014

I HAD a couple of drinks last night and the duvet is on lengthways on the bed which means I can see my toes. So naturally, and I think this is pretty obvious, I got to thinking as to why there aren't any nude beaches in Ireland.

The weather has a lot to with it but not in the way you might think. Here's a warning now: if you are against words like penis and vagina, give up reading and don't be writing letters to my boss telling him I'm a pervert and there's no place in a family newspaper for penises and vaginas.

Read on then my friends but only if you're able for it.

You might say the weather is against the nude beaches. The weather doesn't stop us going to the beaches fully clothed but our climate does have a major influence on us men keeping on our swimming trunks.

Here's why, and you'd nearly have to be a man to understand this. The male member is prone to shrinkage when exposed to the cold.

The sea is not warm at this time of the year and so if a man goes in to the water naked, and comes out naked, well then his manhood will have shrivelled, thereby causing him embarrassment and loss of face.

So there you'd be after coming out of the cold water with your manhood downsized by the cold and you meet the woman from next door, who tells all the neighbours you're a pathetic figure of a man and then every time you take a walk down the street, or go for the paper, and someone gets a fit of laughing, you think they're laughing at you, when they could in fact be laughing at something else altogether.

The unfairness of it is that the post-swim replica doesn't give a true representation of the actual size. It's like buying one of those souvenir statues of the Eiffel Tower.

A few years back, there was an attempt made to turn The Nuns' Strand in Ballybunion into a nude beach. The council were against it and that was that. The Nuns' Strand is at the bottom of a steep cliff, just down from the convent. In the old days, the beach was exclusively for the nuns. You could be excommunicated if you went anywhere near the place when the nuns were bathing.

My friend Maurice Stack will be 97 soon enough and he told me the nuns were dressed from head to toe in layered, black swimsuits.

Four score years ago and more, Maurice and his pals crabbed down along a steep cliff and hid behind a mound covered by the few hardy summer flowers that survive on the cliff face.

They had a good view of the nuns. There was no shortage of nuns back then and about 50 of the sisters walked gingerly out in to the waves. They held hands as a precaution against being swept away. The human daisy chain waded out to just above the knee and then they stopped on the instructions of the Reverend Mother who was supervising from the beach.

The rogue wave hit the 50 nuns simultaneously around the middle parts and all 50 shrieked at the same time. The Reverend Mother ordered the nuns to come back in immediately.

We've come a long way but Irish people have never embraced nudity like, say, the Germans, who are mad for going naked in mixed saunas.

Maybe the influence of the cruel old church that kept the poor nuns in purdah in some way conditions our behaviour today, but probably not. Most of us wouldn't be that bothered by what some mad oul' cardinal would have to say about our morality. Most of our priests are even more liberal than their parishioners. I think the real reasons are the cold and the fact that everyone here in Ireland knows each other. Ireland is too small for secret nudity.

But we'll chance it alright when we go out foreign. There's a big, long nude beach in Masapalomas in Gran Canaria and I met this naked couple from home there a few years back.

She folded her arms and crossed her legs. There I was in my Listowel Emmets' football togs on a nude beach and I could read her thoughts like as if they were written above her head on one of those signs they use for show-ing the scores in golf.

"Isn't it hard luck all the same to meet that bollix here and he'll surely put it in the paper." And I did, but we'll keep the names out of it. Not that there's any-thing to be ashamed of. Her husband saved the day. He looked up at the cloudless sky and said: "I wonder will we get a drop of rain." And off we went in opposite directions.

If we were Swedes or Germans, we'd have gone for an ice-cream.

There's nothing wrong with naked. We should not be ashamed of our own bodies and countless people have suffered from low self-esteem, leading to terrible conditions such as bulimia and anorexia.

It's time we Irish took off our clothes in public to show solidarity with those who are suffering so much. The message is our bodies are one of works of art created by a divine sculptor who broke the mould every time he carved one of us humans, so ensuring an endless variety of body shapes.

I hate that beach in Masapalomas, though. It's full of pervy oul' lads admiring themselves; shaded peeping Toms wearing caps with frontal flaps; and hirsute women from countries where there must be a tax on waxing.

Then there's all these little fish swimming around in schools. I'd be afraid they'd take a nibble like their carnivorous cousins that spend their days in pedicure fish tanks gnawing away at corns and carbuncles.

39

Majestic Day Out At
Ascot A Rite Of Passage

June 19, 2010

I DIDN'T even know he was the Queen's bodyguard. We had been held up in the Royal Enclosure while herself was on her way to the Royal Box. I was eventually let through when Her Majesty was safely in the inner sanctum.

I couldn't see where I was going, what with all these giants with tall hats walking in front of me. The flow landed me accidentally at the Queen's front door. I was almost in when this tall man turned and said ever so politely but with some authority: "You are not expected."

It was the Queen's loss and, yes, I am big headed. My top hat didn't fit. I was getting headaches. Anne and Steve Barry from Knockanure lent me a tall headpiece. Thanks too to Cathal and Mary Henigan from Listowel for the lovely digs.

The day out was all good. Darina Allen was on the plane and she produced goat's cheese on brown bread with little tiny tomatoes like those red snooker balls that flew off the mini- table on Christmas Day and landed in the turkey soup.

We were greeted by green baize-clad ex-soldiers at

the gates of Royal Ascot. I was stopped from going in the Royal Gate. They must have known the grandmother was in Cumann na mBan. Coincidentally, it happened to be Ladies' Day.

The women of England were beautifully togged out.

The Royal Enclosure dresses are just above the knee. Thousands of beauties lie out in The Front Lawn. The skirts here are hitched higher and it was plain to see, even though we weren't looking, the women wore under-wear to match their outfits.

The crowds go right up to about a half a mile from the winning post and the further away you go from the finish the shorter the skirts. By the time you get to the four-furlong marker, the entire collection wouldn't keep a bicycle saddle dry.

There is the delicious waft of perfume all over Ascot. This place is fragrant and floral. It is the colour and the scent of summer.

I was more or less going to slag off the pompous and the slappers, but Royal Ascot is really special. The vary-ing entry levels reflect what was, and still is, the differ-ent tiers of society within a manufactured class system designed to sustain an empire, but I can honesty say I encountered no snobbery or loutishness.

Brough Scott explained it to us: "It's a mix of royalty, fashion and racing. And the racing is very good here."

This year's Ascot Gold Cup was one of the finest races we have ever seen. You just had to be there to appreciate the duel in the hot summer sun between Dermot Weld's Rite Of Passage and Aidan O'Brien's Age Of Aquarius. They battled side by side, neck and neck, sticks like pistons, heels kicking, thighs squeezing, with 40,000 punters cheering as if they had backed them both, even though most didn't.

There was no let-up. Murtagh on Aquarius hit the front a long way out. He knew he had to turn the last few furlongs into a long-distance sprint that would suck the oxygen from his pursuers. Smullen on Rite was calm in his head, manic yet controlled in his drive. Murtagh too gave his all without losing his rhythm.

Age Of Aquarius fought back to briefly lead with the line in sight. Then Rite Of Passage, game and classy, got back in front, barely.

After two and a half miles of no let-up, the length of a horse's neck decided who would lift the 2010 Ascot Gold Cup.

Aquarius and Rite are progressive horses. They will surely meet again in the autumn and many more times. These long-distance champions are only sent to stud when the mileage is up. This is the start of what could become one of racing's great rivalries.

Afterwards, Weld said he took on the triumphant Rite Of Passage because he liked her grandmother and that Melbourne was on the agenda.

"That was some race," we said.

"Ah yeah," replied Weld. Short words, but the 'a' in the 'ah' and the 'ah' in the 'yeah' stretched out like the Curragh.

There was communal singing after the racing in a grassy amphitheatre under the stands to the sound of the Band of the Royal Grenadiers. Some 5,000 people waved miniature Union Jacks and sang 'Land of Hope and Glory', but it was Ireland's day.

Champagne and bacon and egg pies were served from trunks in the car park when the bars closed. Women danced barefooted to car stereos and men shed their tails. I saw a slender girl drink pink champagne out of a fat man's hat.

We met Kieren Fallon, who beat the Queen's horse by a short head, and welcomed him back from his ban.

Mick Channon was surrounded by fans and we sampled his hospitality under an old oak as evening shadows brought a new beauty.

A well-heeled woman on stiletto stilts lost her hat as the wind picked up. She was jarred and couldn't bend down. The feathers ran away from her like a chicken trying to escape the pot and she fell over in the pursuit.

Her legs went up in the air, perpendicular to the grass, with left parallel to right like goalposts. And guess what? She was wearing down-to-the-knee Union Jack passion-killer panties.

The Irish won, but this was a very British day. A day that you should all sample if you get the chance, but please, send word to Her Majesty you are on your way.

40

In Long-Johns And Bundee's Bodhrán Led The Way On Memorable Weekend

March 19, 2018

THE weather was so cold the polar bears in London zoo wore long-johns and the penguins donned a second pair of socks. So did Jonathan Sexton's dad.

I'm staying with Jerry Sexton, the smartest rugby man of them all. Even still, he shocked us with the long-johns. He went for the cowboy-in-the-bunkhouse look.

His son — my godson — is quiet and unbearably modest, but when he togs out, his stated aim is to turn every scuffle into a war.

Jonathan's nana, Brenda, sold a lovely floral dress at half-time. She is 88 and a half.

Clare, his mother, left her hair salon in Dublin's Rathgar just in time for the kick-off. His best friend Laura is expecting their third in three years — the second Sexton Triple Crown in the one season. She minds her husband too.

These mighty women made him. The best players need the best back-up.

Jonathan is only dying to get home to his lovely little family.

He has brains too. There are times when he can barely lift up the kids. But you can't take the fighter out of the boy, for that is who he is, and it is the fight that defines him. Le drop against France won us the Slam. Every man stood up. And whisper it, for once, we had the luck of the Irish.

In Twickenham, our team lit a fire under England right from the go.

The English rugby people were embarrassed by the remarks of their coach, who referenced the "scummy Irish". Eddie Jones is in the last act of a one-man Shakespearian tragedy. His scummy Irish and anti-Welsh comments were no more than boxing trash talk. Eddie, I'm told, likes us.

Who should I meet but Conor Murray's mother Barbara, and this is what I said to her: "There's one favour I need Barbara: is there any chance you could have another baby?"

The players were too tired to celebrate in the team hotel. You would swear they lost. The English were bigger and they hit hard.

We cheered and we cried and we gloried on a white St Patrick's Day in London. The Slam is won for only the third time since the death of our patron saint in 432 AD. That's only the bare three in about 1,700 years of Patrick's Days.

These young men knew. They knew their games were the lifting of a nation and the making of new history.

But yesterday our heroes cut loose in Heathrow when the plane was delayed. Bundee Aki made a bodhrán out of a tray. He is as Irish now as any of us. They sang The Fields at the tops of their voices. And I gave them a hand.

Teacher Joe sat back. Boys will be boys.

We as a country owe so much to Joe. Joe is an organiser and, like all good teachers, he is firm but fair. His hard work is the key to success, not just in sport, but in every walk of life and is the template for a better Ireland.

We have the courage and the intelligence. All we need to grow stronger as a country is to work on the detail. Joe looks after the small stuff.

But there's more. He is creative too. This year we played the running game and scored more tries than ever before.

Joe coached his school and he knows boys move on. Our headmaster is building for the future. The finishing 10, 12, and 13 are only barely past shaving age.

Ah but it's good to be Irish, both new and old. We're a fair old place all the same, aren't we? For the size of us, or for any size. And now one size fits all.

Young boys and young girls will take confidence and courage from the thinking and the doing. Old boys and old girls, from an Ireland that was often down on self-confidence, pay homage to an Ireland that will survive and thrive.

There are no boundaries to the march of our nation. We used to be only a small place just clinging on. But our boys lifted a tiny nation to the exalted and the glorious.

This publicity lark isn't really Brian's style. But after weeks of agonising, he felt he had to go public to give thanks, and to encourage those who are worried about the future.

41

Heartfelt Thanks After 25
Years Of A New Ticker

February 18, 2017

BRIAN JAFFRAY'S new heart was stitched in to his chest 25 years and a few days ago. Brian isn't quite sure exactly who is the longest surviving heart transplant patient in Ireland, but he's right up there.

Now a quarter of a century on since his life was saved by a person he never met, Brian wants to thank the man or woman who gave him the chance to get married and have kids. His harvested heart was a gift from a family who somehow managed to find clear thinking time for love and giving in their darkest days. I can only imagine how tough it was back then for those who lost a loved one.

That one heart gave life to five lives. Brian was just 28 when he was saved and he was a single man. Brian's wife Caroline and sons Daniel, Eoin and Andrew are a family thanks to a family.

This publicity lark isn't really Brian's style. But after weeks of agonising, he felt he had to go public to give thanks, and to encourage those who are worried about the future.

In he goes for the last 25 years to the Heart and Lung Transplant Unit in The Mater, with his head down, and he's plugged in to his ear phones.

Brian hardly looks up at the other patients waiting for their news. It's his way of coping. "It may seem as if I'm ignoring the other survivors. I hardly ever even think of the fact that I have a second heart. Most people don't even know. Some haven't been lucky. This can go wrong. Thinking about it too much can get to you."

It has always been this way. Brian had an operation for a hole in his heart when he was a kid but his parents made sure their son had a normal upbringing.

He played football and rugby in his beloved Tullamore, where he lives now after a stint in Dublin.

We are good friends. When I started off writing here 17 years ago, Brian gave me the confidence I lacked. I came from a family of literary high achievers and never spent so much as a day in journalism college. So there I was loading my insecurities on Brian and I never knew he had plenty to think about himself.

Independent News & Media's head of sports content Dave Courtney tells of Brian's "consummate professionalism. I would describe him as a journalist's journalist". Brian has what the London taxi drivers describe as "The Knowledge". And there was always empathy, but with an eagle eye out for errors.

Brian came back to Tullamore from Dublin to look after his elderly parents, who have since passed on. He was always a Tullamore boy. Home is now where his heart is. It was payback time. His mother and father minded the little boy with the hole in his heart so well. Brian now works at his own business as a communications and social media consultant. He specifically asked me not to mention that. So there Brian, it's now my turn to edit you.

I was in Brian's house one time and got to nosing about. There was a framed newspaper page in an alcove off the hallway. That was when I found out. Brian wrote a beautiful piece when he was saved. The first lines read: "I could count the remaining days of my life by flicking through three pages of a calendar. March, April, May... RIP. I was dying."

Our then editor Vinnie Doyle called to The Mater to see Brian. "There I was lying on my back, with tubes stuck in everywhere, and there was the boss getting me to write a piece. I was delighted to be asked as it meant there would be no petting or mollycoddling. I think Vinnie knew that was what I needed at that time."

He wrote of the 26-year-old him, waiting for the call for the transplant, wondering and wasting. Two years it took, with false alarms and heart rejections in between, and he was only given a year to live. Brian was still just a young lad and he never let his problem get in the way of a good time. The young Jaffray used to switch off the bleeper from the Mater transplant people when he went to Bad Bob's Backstage Bar "in case I got lucky".

The humour, too, sustained him. His old sports editor, PJ Cunningham, recalls how it was that people "queued up to be insulted by him ... only they are not real insults, just little put downs that somehow make you feel better. That is his gift".

His cardiologist, the late Brian Maurer, was like a father to the young boy and then man. Surgeon Freddy Wood looked at Brian's old heart after the transplant. It was three times the normal size. "The size of a cow's heart," he said.

Brian wrote from the ticker. "These were the glorious opening moments of a new life. Hang in there, heart."

Nowadays Brian is being looked after by his GP, Dr David Bartlett, and Professor Jim O'Neill who is an Offaly man. "I'm so lucky to be minded so well by such fine people. It's more than a job. They really care."

Caroline was with Brian when the beeper went off 25 years ago. She's a Donegal woman and is not one for giving up. "I was always treated as just a husband and a father. There are days when I get down. Caroline is always there with the daily resurrection. I owe it to the person who died that I might live to make the most out of the life he or she never had. I don't even know if I would be able to meet the family. I just want them to know I'm doing well."

Today at noon in the chapel in the Mater, Brian Jaffray will attend his 25th Mass in honour of those who gave life to so many. And on every year of the previous 24, Brian lit a candle.

He will light another today and say a little prayer too for a person he never knew, and a family he never met, who gave him a second shot at life. Brian, my friend, you have honoured their love and generosity. Happy 25th, heart.

42

Shame On World Rugby
For Putting Money First

November 6, 2017

WORLD Rugby placed Ireland third of three. World Rugby didn't get the value of bringing rugby back to the people.

World Rugby went for the money. And rich bums on pricey seats will replace families and fans who care.

World Rugby has no memory. World Rugby has no loyalty. They have forgotten our contribution to the game. Ireland has never hosted a World Cup. And unless the rugby-playing nations come to our aid, no small country, including New Zealand, will ever host a World Cup again.

World Rugby has no sense of fun. The sterile report never referenced an Ireland of storytellers, an Ireland of the party and the good times to come. World Rugby has no heart.

The country that paid the most won. World Rugby sold out.

Ireland's World Cup bid, under the excellent leadership of Dick Spring who gave three years of his life to the cause, were never told of any concerns regarding huge all-seater stadia at the beginning the bid process.

There was a secret and the secret was World Rugby wanted big loads of money. Sometimes silence can be as misleading as the spoken word. But we still met their price of €120 million.

The report that condemned Ireland was a box-ticking exercise. The country with the most money was always going to win.

Our infrastructure is more than adequate. We guarantee packed houses in every well-resourced, atmospheric venue — at affordable prices.

Killarney rivals any tourism town anywhere in the world. The lakes and mountains are a wonder of the world. Indeed there are more tourists here in August than will ever come to the World Cup.

Billy Beaumont's men must have called at night. There was a concern expressed in the report that the old and historic Fitzgerald Stadium needs work.

This is Killarney, a place where things get built and built quickly. It's not as if the World Cup will be held next week or even next year. We have six years to do the work.

Perversely, World Rugby is critical of new and lustrous Páirc Uí Chaoimh. There was work to be done, they said.

It's done Billy, but no one checked. Páirc Uí Chaoimh can easily be turned in to an all- seater but for many of us the terracing makes for a better atmosphere. And it makes for cheaper tickets. And it's safe Billy. Very safe.

And Cork will be full, Billy. Cork will rock. We are a people's people, Billy. And a nation of welcomes. There was no mention of that either in the report.

Ireland can cater for all attendances. Thomond Park takes 26,000 and will be full for every game in the most fervent rugby town anywhere.

World Rugby wanted everyone sitting down. As at a dinner party so they can fleece the picnic people and therefore charge more for the food and beer franchises.

Dan Carter described Thomond Park in these terms: "Wasn't the result we were after but on a personal level it was amazing to finally play at the legendary Thomond Park. Wow, what an atmosphere."

Leinster played a few weeks ago in a big stadium in South Africa. The 3,000 present were lost in the concrete. The locals, good people that they are, will not be able to afford the prices.

Did you know the price of tickets for The Lions Tour to NZ was around €350?

Most of the people going to games won't even understand the rules while the kids and the coaches will be watching on TV, if they can afford the channels, seeing as TV is propping up the obscene anti-family South African and French money buy-offs.

It is universally acknowledged that Dublin is the best place on earth for a rugby international. The big stadia are in the city centre.

Dublin is well able to cope with a succession of 80,000 sell-outs as is evidenced every summer during the GAA season. Every Dub will be an ambassador for the funniest city in the world.

Moss Keane was a friend of mine. I helped write his book. Moss Keane was a friend of Billy Beaumont's. Billy partied in Dublin with Moss. He knows who we are and why we are the way we are.

Moss Keane said "there is no border in an Irish dressing room". Rugby was an all-Ireland sport during the worst of The Troubles and it still is.

Now north and south have united behind the Irish bid. The unity of minds, of people and of purpose, will have a lasting benefit. World Rugby have placed the money men before the peacemakers.

We have never hosted a World Cup. France and South

Africa have had their turn. The lack of empathy here is appalling.

World Rugby made it clear South Africa is ahead of us in experience.

Ireland welcomes millions of tourists every year. Many more than the World Cup's 450,000 come here in August alone. This is easy for us. We can do the World Cup without any fuss.

World Rugby, believe it or not, placed South Africa ahead of Ireland in terms of security.

I dearly love South Africa. The people there rival us in terms of the friendliness, warmth and welcome but South Africa is a very dangerous place.

The latest South African crime report published a month ago by their police covers the period from the April 1, 2016 to March 31, 2017.

There were 608,321 contact crimes which include murder, attempted murder rape, sexual offences, hijacking, serious assaults and muggings. There is a huge problem in South Africa with the under-reporting of crime.

You would worry if World Rugby were asked to assess the picking of a lollipop person at the school gate.

The French bid expressed the hope there would be hardly any terrorism by 2023. Even the ostrich looks around every now and then.

I was in Bordeaux last year for soccer's European Championship finals.

There wasn't a police person to be seen on the over-packed tram to the game.

We were checked by a frail man in his seventies before we entered the fan zone in front of the stadium. A big sneeze would have knocked him to the ground.

The rugby security was just as bad in Stade de France. We warned of this here in these pages before a terror attack outside the stadium which could have killed hundreds but for a lucky break.

Just a month ago a bomb was found outside Parc des Princes in Paris before a soccer game. France is under a state of emergency. And they tell us France is safe.

There is one last vote. We are a mighty nation who will not be found wanting. No one will be stuck for a bed or a dinner.

This is Ireland of the welcomes and we see it as our patriotic duty to mind our visitors like we would our own families.

Please vote for Ireland, her people and your people. Please vote for the kids and their wide-eyed wonder. Please vote for the underdog. We will not let you down.

**One question was:
Why was Guinness black?
I didn't know, even though I've
been selling and drinking the
stuff for all of my adult life.**

43

Gripping Yarns From A Wet Summer's Day In A Co Kerry Pub

September 14, 2015

DID you know there are women living in the high peaks of somewhere in Pakistan who never get the menopause? The result is that the women who live in the highlands can have babies until they are well into their eighties.

I'm not too sure if this amazing 'fact' is true or not, and I didn't bother to check it out.

But the man who told me of the mountainy older mothers was in no way unsure of his own abilities. I was stretched out on one of the seats of our pub, waiting for the next wave of customers.

In the days before Listowel races, customers come in waves of one.

He came very close, close enough to kiss. The man who knew all the interesting facts.

"Move back, man," I said. "I need my space." I've always hated when people put their face in to mine.

Later I realised the man was slightly deaf and needed to get close so that he could get his hearing aid near to my lips.

I was sorry then for pushing him away. On another day, I almost barred a man with MS when he staggered into the pub and had trouble ordering as his voice had been slowed down by his condition.

Something told me to hold on for a second, and I did.

The man who invaded my facial space told me he had travelled quite a bit and he was shouting out quite loud, presumably so he could hear himself speak.

He presented the interesting facts by way of asking questions, which had two results — the first was to prove how much he knew and the second was to show how little I knew.

One question was: Why was Guinness black? I didn't know, even though I've been selling and drinking the stuff for all of my adult life.

The answer, he said, had something to do with hops, and then he told me about the women in Pakistan.

He moved off when my cousins from Cork came into the pub and they told me of a very, very interesting fact that had to do with a description of the size of a man's member.

Before we get on to the descriptive, we will stick with the narrative for a little while.

All these fascinating stories were told to me last Friday when the rains came and refused to leave. All day long it poured, and I was in the pub all day long.

Phil, who has worked with us for years, had to go home. Her beautiful house was flooded, up to the windows, when a bog canal burst its banks.

Phil was my mother's pal. As if she wasn't devastated enough from the passing of the mother. But she got on with it.

The fire brigade couldn't even get into the house as the water inside and outside were at the same level.

So I told her about the man who told me of the women in Pakistan. You couldn't keep Phil down.

Herself and the mother used to go on shopping trips and very often they would come back without buying anything, which gave them great satisfaction in that they saved so much.

But this was a terrible blow.

So I'm in the bar when I shouldn't be and in come the Cork cousins and their story of penile calibration.

It seems there was a man from their parts who had the name of having a particularly large member.

By way of a point of information, I think I should point out for foreign people and those of you who have never discussed or heard tell of such matters concerning or pertaining to the male appendage that "member" is the Irish word for penis.

We don't like to use such expressions in public, though, so from now on we will use the word "member." If you don't mind.

So it seems someone in a pub somewhere in Cork asked the man with the large member if his member was as big as was rumoured and, if it was, well then exactly how big or long was it.

"'Tis that long," said the man with the large member, "that 11 robins could perch upon it in a row, although to be fair, the one at the end might have to stand on one leg."

Later in the day, Phil called to say they had managed to get the water out of the house.

The tide marks were everywhere and poor Phil had only just redecorated the house a few months ago for her son' s wedding.

Her friends in the bar were devastated. Mickey MacConnell has been a good pal of Phil's for a good many years.

Mickey composed 'Only Our Rivers Run Free', and they ran in to Phil's house.

Like all great entertainers, Mickey can read a room, so by way of cheering us up he told us the following true story.

Mickey was gigging in Ballybunion last weekend and he took a break to smoke a cigarette with his musical accomplice, the accomplished Wayne Taren.

This American lady asked Mickey what was the name of their band. Mickey and Wayne hadn't quite got around to naming their band, so Mickey looked behind the rather large lady and spotted a brown road sign for The Wild Atlantic Way.

"Our band," said Mickey, "is called The Wild Atlantic Way."

"Gee," went the American lady, "you guys must be famous, I've seen signs advertising your band all over Ireland."

Phil, up to her ankles in water, had a good laugh at that one. So goes an ordinary Friday in the very ordinary life of a small town barman.

Leaving Cert Season: An Endurance Test For The Whole Family

April 13, 2015

THE Leaving Cert season is upon us again, now that Easter is over.

The pressure will be boiling over. Mothers will be making special soups made from lentils and goodness vegetables to build up the students. Fathers will be driving to daily grinds and pop-up revision courses.

The Nana will burn more wax in the church than the quality control department in Madame Tussauds and the grandfather's annual Leaving Cert dream will see him kicking the duvet up to the ceiling from involuntary leg movements brought on by the trickiness of question 7 in the Maths Paper 2, of 1953.

The only good thing to be said about The Leaving is that it ends.

Parents suffer just as much anxiety as the kids. And more. Many parents are like Hollywood mothers and live their wasted youth all over again, vicariously through their kids.

I seem to have read somewhere about the father who went looking for the person who set the hard Maths 2 or English 1, or it could have been Irish 1 and English 2, all of which sound suspiciously like the results of a group of death in the European Championship.

The father was going to do the question setter a good deal of harm, he said.

Many fathers are Hollywood mothers. They blame the fact they haven't a clue what the kids are studying on the poor teachers.

The Leaving never leaves us. I still get the Leaving Dreams. So maybe I imagined the whole thing about the crazed father hunting down the paper setters because his kid's poet didn't come up.

Only the other day, I met a man who was in school with me, and a great shock it was too, for I was at his funeral during last year's Leaving Cert. I had this vague feeling that we prayed for him no end and gave him the usual praise reserved only for the dead.

But it must have been a dream because my old school companion asked me for the loan of a twenty, which reminded me that he was a serial tapper in the old days. It could well be that the inner accountant in me killed him off.

The worst thing is that the Leaving Cert dreams last even longer than the bloody exams, which go on forever, particularly if the students are studying Applied Aramaic or some obscure subject.

I haven't seen him since, the tapper I killed off in the dream. The twenty was worth it to be rid of him. He was hard going, always on about how smart he was, with stunning facts like how many eggs a cricket could lay, even though we all knew there wasn't a hope of crickets coming up in Biology.

The Leaving isn't the place for those who store up useless information.

Apart from the fact that you'll get no one to sit near

you in the pub when you grow into full adulthood, the results will suffer in a direct ratio to the amount of useless information stored in your head.

The Leaving is a ruthless business. It's all about results. And the parents' job is like that of a football coach. We must provide the optimum conditions for the mind athletes to excel. Emotional support and love go a long way but getting the logistics right is equally important. The exam must be planned like a military operation.

I often feel parents do not take this side of the education of their kids seriously enough.

There will be lows in most exams, a day when the student feels it hasn't gone quite right. So you tell your charge to lock the bad day up in a box and move on to the next one. This is the way Ronan O'Gara and Jonathan Sexton operate. When they miss a kick, they banish the mistake to another, far-away place, and kick the next one between the posts.

The Department of Education has the Leaving Cert students playing against the wind in both halves. Here's the schedule for a young lad whose mother contacted us. The Leaving Certificate Oral Tests are to be held from April 13 to April 24, and the main exam starts in June.

The orals are right in the middle of the key revision. The boy is good at languages and so he has three orals to contend with in the space of a couple of weeks. He's trying to finish a history project. Another lad has an engineering submission, an agricultural science project and two orals.

Why is it these exams, which could well shape the future of a young person's career, cannot be staggered? Some of the practicals could be completed before Christmas. The Leaving has become a test of endurance. The pressure is too much, too soon and so it is not a fair test.

But it's on now and the students have to make the most of the time left.

Parents have to think their way through the exams. Be kind, careful and make life easier for your kids. You may have to put up with the occasional Leaving Cert tantrum.

There's life after Leaving. My Dad failed first time around and now they're studying his plays for the exams. But he did repeat, and passed the following year.

45

There Are Lessons For All Of Us As Little Ones Start School

August 28, 2012

SHE'LL take to the bed at 10 and wonder where the years have gone. Not her years but the five or so belonging to her little baby who went off to school today for the very first time.

Even though you know your little boy will be home in a couple of hours, the pillow is wet with tears.

The teacher seemed nice enough and the boys and girls were fine even if the blond girl who sat next to your baby kissed him on the cheek.

"They're all bitches only your mom," you feel like telling him. You know then you're being obsessive and possessive.

You realise these little kids will be his friends forever. You wonder who will be the closest ones as you scan the class.

In a few years the close ones will walk into your kitchen and help themselves to the contents of the fridge and it will not bother you in the least because they are his friends and will always be, for such it is with the kids you start out with. All reared out of the one pot and as much an influence on your child's life as anyone he is ever likely to meet in the years ahead.

It was so long ago but I have this vague recollection of my Dad taking me up Courthouse Road -- my mother was too heartbroken to bring me on that first day -- and there he was, Mickeen Carey, up on a ladder, painting a house at his ease.

Mickeen had a cat named Tibbles who could meow the 'Cliffs of Dooneen' in Japanese.

Mickeen's face was full of sympathy. It was a last look at the old order. Somehow I sort of knew I was being launched out into a great voyage.

That's all I remember. Mrs Scanlan our teacher was nice. I know that much, but other than that last look at Mickeen I cannot remember a single day in Babies.

It's as if I was in a coma and missed a year of my life.

You live so much longer if you keep a diary. It's all there to be read back over when memory fades and reality turns into myth as the years pass by.

The mammy or daddy might keep one until the son grows older and then he can carry on. The entries will spark recollection and your child will live twice over.

The other tip for the first timers is to start sparing now for college. Time flies as the man said when it took him two seconds to scroll through six months on the online airline calendar. That's how it is.

If you are grieving today, cheer up, for you too will make lifelong friends, especially if you are living far away from your native place. Up until school the mammy will feel lonely for her female companionship and then through meetings at school gates she too will develop lasting friendships. But here's a cautionary tale told to me by the principal of a big school in Belfast.

The father arrived back from his travels with a lovely bride from the Far East. She was shy but willing, both in the bedroom and in the kitchen. The tradition in her country was the woman was to do her man's bidding, no matter what. The husband was a decent sort and he loved her very much. He offered to do his share of the housework.

One day he got up from the kitchen table to fetch a tablespoon and his beautiful, elfin, dusky bride was most upset he didn't ask her to get the spoon.

She collected their child every day after school while the hunter gatherer was off out in the city earning money at his desk.

Bit by bit the eastern beauty became friends with the other school mothers. At her husband's insistence the perfect wife invited her new friends over for Eastern pastries so sweet and light and full of intricate, subtle flavours she never had any bother in persuading her guests to come back for afters.

The Eastern lady made many friends. After a time it could truly be said she became more Irish than the Irish themselves. Now he does his own ironing and the banker's chauvinistic friend tells him it was the bitches at the school gate who got to her.

Education is not just for kids. Mammies learn too.

You get up in the unusual stillness and blow dry his duck down pillow with a hairdryer in case the new scholar somehow cops you've been crying.

A watched clock never ticks but somehow it crawls to hometime.

Then as you wait outside the school the lollipop lady, sweating like a sumo under her big yellow coat, swears all kids are psychopaths who pay no attention to the safe-cross or any other code and you worry if you've sent him to the right school.

You tell her you've considered home schooling but you were afraid you wouldn't be able to do the maths.

The lollipop lady tells you one and one is still two as she bats a butterfly over the school wall with her big sign.

The bell rings and you rush in as quickly as Katie Taylor.

This is the first of many school reports. Maybe teacher will say your lad is a genius and they're putting him into secondary school straight away. Maybe he failed Lego.

Your heart pounds and it will pound many times over the coming years on the mornings of Leaving Certs and college exams.

He will cuddle up to you at the end of that first day when you get home. You feel reassured. He says he doesn't want to go back. It's not easy for a little boy so used to one on one, to learn how to handle one on 21.

"How long does school go on for mammy?" he asks trustingly. You haven't the heart to tell him he has nearly 20 years to go. He's a lifer now.

Soon you will have to go back to work. Another parting. You've toiled and thought your way to get where you are now and your career is important. The money is needed to pay bills and it's only a small consolation that there are many more mammies in exactly the same situation. But you will manage, somehow, as best you can.

You read for him, the best education of all. Soon he falls asleep in your arms, exhausted from the first day. And his little sleepy head, teeming with new ideas, even in dreamtime, rests lightly on his dried out duck- down pillow.

46

Kerry Candles Will Burn Bright For Mickey Harte

July 21, 2012

KERRY and Tyrone is so much more than a football match. For Mickey Harte and for all of us.

There will be many even in heartland of the Kingdom who will cheer for Tyrone. The sympathy and affection for Mickey Harte knows no boundaries.

If we're beaten in Killarney this evening, all of us will back Tyrone for the rest of the summer, but for now we will roar for our own beloved Kerry.

Don't tell Mr Ahmed.

Mr Ahmed, a renowned throat specialist, told me a persistent hoarseness was down to mucus seeping from an old battle wound of a broken nose.

Indeed I remember the blow only too well. It was at a carnival game in Moyvane, the Rio of north Kerry. The murderous corner-back who hit me with a kango of an elbow declared it was all a terrible accident -- it was my brother Conor he was after.

This evening we will do our best to keep quiet, but championship fervour has ruined more throats than Woodbines.

All of Ireland will cheer themselves hoarse for Mickey Harte.

He knows what it takes to beat Kerry. This will be four in a row in championship games if Tyrone win.

Tyrone desperately crave victory on our sacred turf and a win by playing classy football. Once that first All-Ireland was wrought from a mix of graft, guts, skill and puke too, Mickey has always kept an eye on the history of style.

Tyrone will try to run Kerry off the pitch and out the gate up into the Macgillicuddy Reeks, a well-known retreat for a beaten Kerry team.

Referee Dave Goldrick has a tough job. Goldrick is one of the best refs in the game, despite the occasional human lapse. He is also one of the fairest and has no favourites.

But now Dave has to referee a saga of a game between the two fiercest rivals in the GAA, and the background is everyone everywhere would love for Tyrone to win this one.

All we want is fair play. Yes we did get a refereeing break against Westmeath in Mullingar last Sunday, but that was as rare as a sunny day in summer.

The neutrals for Tyrone among you will claim I am biased.

Yes I am Kerry and always will be. I will not join in the criticism of our team and manager.

When I started to write this column more than 10 years ago, I promised I would never down my own county.

We are up against it this evening. There isn't much confidence behind the team within Kerry. Gallant Westmeath were desperately unlucky. Kerry only played for 10 minutes but I believe we can win, if we multiply 10 by seven.

Kerry are seldom underdogs. It's almost a luxury for us.

Never mind the bookies. Their odds are accountancy-based, to offset the flood of money on Kerry to win the All-Ireland.

In the hearts and minds of Kerry people, Tyrone are hot favourites. Yet Kerry have always given their best when they are unfancied.

Our friend Kieran Donaghy, of Tyrone ancestry, has been written off by those two well-known footballers on the ditch, all and sundry. Expect a big game from the big man this evening, for that's the nature of the fierce pride in jersey and self that epitomises the hero from Tralee town.

I'm sure Mickey Harte would approve of such loyalty. He has played with and managed county and club for all of his life.

No man has ever been more welcome in our county.

He will, as usual, stand quietly by the edge of the dugout with a cognitive finger under his jaw as he calmly analyses the fury before him.

Part of his magic as a manager is that he distances himself from time and place. But I am sure there are long nights when Mauritius is only too near and January is today.

Mickey would swap every All-Ireland ever played for one hour with his beloved Michaela but that will come too, in time, and many more hours with it. And that will be the joyous meeting.

We are torn in Kerry by an undying loyalty to the Kingdom and the love and respect we hold for this mighty man who in so many ways has brought such dignity and honour to his beloved Tyrone and has inspired all of us, in every jersey.

Mickey must keep the tragedy that befell his lovely daughter separate from football. He has to, but the goodwill and sympathy we all carry for the bereaved families has become an intrinsic part of the emotional conscious-ness of a nation.

There will be candles burning brightly in Kerry win-dows tonight to light Mickey and Tyrone safely home and a prayer will be said in every green and gold Kerry heart for the Hartes and McAreaveys.

Yes this is more than a game. It is a manifestation of solidarity and sympathy for two GAA families torn by events outside of their control.

Two families we in the GAA desperately desire to put back together again.

47

Chair A Symbol Of Hope
For Women Given Help To
Rebuild Their Broken Lives

April 1, 2017

THERE I was, alone in the sitting room where broken lives are fixed, and stories never told before are told for the first time.

The half-painted baby chair caught my eyes. The chair seemed out of place. A pony standing in among giraffes. It was like the chair in 'Goldilocks and the Three Bears'. Scattered here and there were more broken and half-fixed chairs in various states of repair and decoration. The little kiddies chair, I thought, is probably being made up as a present, or something like that.

Even now, three days on, I can hardly write about the story behind the small chair.

The tea was being made and I was trying to get a feel for the energy in the sitting room in the Kerry Rape and Sexual Abuse Centre in Tralee. The room was no different to your living room at home. It was homely and cushiony. And bright, welcoming and warm too, in the spring sunshine, on the best day since last October.

Some rooms send out their own biography. The sitting room where so many tears were shed was transmitting a message of hope, love and of light.

I pictured a young person, a girl, in my mind's eye. I could see her sitting there on the sofa, nervous and barely able to speak. She has been raped. That's what I picked up there in the living room. Even as I write now I can see the hunched abstract outline of a real girl I never met.

Vera O'Leary is the director here. Vera has been helping to mend these broken lives for 25 years. This year is the 25th year of the centre.

I'm guessing you are like me in that you cannot listen to or read any more accounts of the evil done to those who have been abused by members of their own families in particular. So I was dreading the interview. Put it off three times. But I might just skip ahead to the end. I left this place of refuge and healing with the certain feeling there was great hope for the good and the caring.

"Sometimes the victims have to carry a secret. There are no secrets here," Vera said. She emphasised the confidentiality though, as you would expect. "What keeps us going is the determination and belief that any person who has been sexually abused is entitled to a very high standard (of care)."

This is one tough and determined woman, stubborn even, who has fought against old and misshapen attitudes and values. Vera and more like her have helped to mould us in to a more caring race of people. Her fight has changed us Irish men's attitudes towards women for the better, for the most part.

"Twenty five years ago I wouldn't even tell people I was working here. We never told anyone. Now it's all out in the open," she said.

I asked her about the chairs over at the back of the room. "All of the chair makers have been victims of sexual violence," she said.

And it was then I realised the meaning of baby chair.

The woman who was restoring the chair was abused when she was a child. I was unable to respond and had to take time out. Never have I been so affected. There was another bigger chair with a second back melded on to the original. I'm guessing now that the woman who was creating her statement may have been abused by a priest. Another chair had scorpions and bugs painted underneath the seat part.

These women who suffered so much are strong now. All of the women were counselled here. Vera told me of a sisterly togetherness among the women in the sitting room. The chair ladies went through tears and laughter as they painted and planed their pain away.

The chair ladies are the success stories from this ter-raced house of hope and salvation. The plan is for an exhibition later in the year to celebrate the 25th anni-versary.

I'm tough enough but it took tea, several biscuits and Vera's soft words to get me going again. I could not get the small chair out of my head.

"Don't forget to mention the Ring of Kerry cycle," Vera said, ever practical, as she needs to be. "The centre is 70pc State funded and there is no charge for counselling. The people who need us can come back any time they like."

You can register to cycle as part of a fund-raiser for the centre. Do it for the chair ladies.

The work goes on and the problems change and morph.

I came across a beautiful homemade card of thanks from an older lady who was raped.

Vera said the big problem now is the easy accessibility of porn: "Young men who have easy access to porn objec-tify women and put more pressure on girls to behave in a certain way."

The other major problem is that of where consent starts and ends: "We have a programme now for young people which basically explains you must ask for express permission before you go further. It's all about communication."

The financial pressure on the service is constant. There were 60 appointments booked after the revelations in Tuam from abuse survivors, mostly from residential homes. Not one was refused a session.

I didn't want to pry but I just had to ask about the woman who was working on the baby chair. Vera said it's OK. She had permission. The brave woman's aim and that of her chair-making friends was to show others who have been abused that there was a cure there in the sitting room.

"Has she a family of her own?"

"She has," Vera said.

"And is she happy?"

"Yes she is. She's strong now," she added.

And I'm told the maker of the baby chair is a very loving mother.

48

Kingdom Playing For
The Living And The Dead

September 20, 2014

MY grandfather Bill Keane was a primary teacher and he taught in his beloved country school of Clounmacon, just outside Listowel.

Bill was forever thinking up innovative teaching plans, and the thinking took his mind off the long, steep hill he had to scale every morning on his way to class.

Jim McGuinness and Eamonn Fitzmaurice have climbed their own mountains and they will understand the grandfather's desire to keep the lessons fresh. His mission was to bring the best out of his pupils and so it was that Bill put up a prize of a bar of chocolate for the best essay of the day.

Back in those post-war days of rationing, the bar of chocolate was the equivalent of the Booker Prize. The topic for the essay had to be a tough one. The simpler titles like 'A Day at the Seaside', or 'My Dog Spot' wouldn't do at all.

Before we go back to the point, it just dawned on me that if we win tomorrow there will be the usual outbreak of Kerry jokes by way of keeping us in our place. My favourite is, what did the Kerryman call his pet zebra? Spot was the zebra's name.

And here's a new one for you which we have just composed to commemorate the occasion of this the first All-Ireland final between Kerry and Donegal. What name did the Kerryman give to his beloved tortoise? The answer is Rover.

Bill Keane the first, gave out the title for the essay. It was 'The Hawk and the Rat'. There was much head-scratching and the word conundrum was used by mentoring parents on knuckly bohereen, baldy haggard and lush meadow.

It wasn't part of the prize back in 1946, but we will now publish the winning composition. The entire essay comprised just the one line. Here it is: "The hawk is a hoor to fly and the rat is bad article to have around the house."

The footballing qualities and weaknesses of friend and foe will be parsed, and as with the small child who won the bar of chocolate, the trick is to reduce the answers into the succinct.

So what then does it take to win an All-Ireland final? The winners will have to forage, harvest, create little and great masterpieces. There will come a time when the match will turn as surely as the tides of Ballybunion and Bundoran.

Eamonn and Jim are not playing, though, and the players will win the game. For me there is only one tactic and that is get to the ball first. Kerry are good at that. Donegal will try to take the ball off Kerry and counter with speed.

In my lifetime I have never seen a Kerry team so written off so often and by so many. I always knew we would be there or thereabouts. Our boys are ravenously hungry. They will play at a relentless pace and they play the North Kerry way. The Kerry-Mayo game was the most intense match ever. There was no time on the ball and the hits were frequent and ferocious.

Kerry are as fit as they have ever been and I believe the bookies have it wrong. Donegal are hot favourites.

The men from the north-west are every bit as up for the game as we are. Donegal have evolved into an exciting, counterattacking team. Michael Murphy (below) could win the game on his own. Donegal will be well schooled and there will be no lack of courage.

Yet I still think Kerry will win. There are those of us who believe Kerry's name has been inscribed on the broad base of the Sam Maguire ever since we lost in the last minutes to Dublin in that famous semi-final of 2013. The hurt and the sense of loss can either finish off or make up a team.

Kerry rode their luck against valiant Mayo but there was more. In the end Kerry won because we refused to die. We love the infinite gentle friendliness of Donegal and I hope you do not take offence from our praising Kerry but there's no point in feigning mock impartiality. And if Donegal beat us, we will give them due credit here on Monday.

In Kerry, football has been the glory game and it has always been this way. For us there is no purer expression of the love we bear for our native place than the winning of an All-Ireland.

The All-Ireland isn't just played on the third Sunday in September in Croke Park. Our kids play the All-Ireland final several times a day every day. The final is played on by-roads with a Mohican of grass running up the middle and in and out through goal-post front gates in busy urban estates.

Here is a true maternity story. The pregnant Kerry mother feels the kick. She smiles, and says to her partner, "a footballer".

The dad asks "which leg is it?" The mother replies, and this is what she actually said to the father of her child, "I can't see from here."

Later, after the baby bursts out from defence in to the light of day, the child will kick off the blanket in the cot. "A citeoig," the dad will say, "like myself."

It goes from the cradle to the grave.

There is an older Kerry lady in exile, who is half-way between this world and the next. The lady is an excellent judge of literature. She reads this column every week. We called to see her a few weeks back and she's still to the good.

"I'm in the departure lounge," she whispers with a smile. Death holds no fears for her. The wise lady sees her endgame as no more than a portal to a new and enhanced life after life.

The rosary beads are wrapped around her thin fingers as she prays for Kerry. Her weak voice masks a fighting heart. The words spoken are barely audible above the gentle autumn breeze, lilting in through the open window of her bedroom .

"I'm praying Kerry win one more All-Ireland before I go."

You'd think the Kerry woman would be praying for a premium level seat in heaven. The team always comes first.

Donal Walsh, the brave teenager, spent his final days trying to save lives of those who are in danger of dying by suicide. He supported our boys in Croke Park when we last played in an All-Ireland final and now they're backing him. Our senior and minor teams wear his wrist bands, night and day.

Donal is their hero from their own time. The young men of Kerry are loyal to those who have gone before.

The words engraved on the bands are Donal's. "Livelife. A door will open."

Kerry it is then to honour Donal and to give a fitting send-off to the faraway lady playing her last match, in time added on.

The simple cross and tabernacle are her Sistine Chapel but there is another cathedral she longed to visit but was forbidden to do so for so many years, and that was Croke Park.

49

Sister de Sales, Kerry's Football Nun, Knows From A Life Of Hard Work That All-Irelands Are Won In Babies' Class

December 20, 2014

SISTER de Sales is the last of the Dingle nuns. She lives all on her own in the big, old Presentation Convent that was once home to 40 or more sisters.

De Sales has plenty of company. Jesus and the spirits of sisters past are always with her. De Sales speaks as if the spirit world is in the here and now.

"I feel their presence in a very real way. My friends are with me and I pray with them as if we were all living together under the roof on the convent."

The heroes of the western world mind her at night. Dara Ó Cinnéide and Paddy Kennedy are from different generations of Kerry football and De Sales has their photos framed on the walls of the little cell where she goes to sleep every night.

"I will always have Dara and Paddy to look after me," she laughs. De Sales pours the tea in the little room she has made into her own holy place. The simple cross and tabernacle are her Sistine Chapel but there is another cathedral she longed to visit but was forbidden to do so for so many years, and that was Croke Park.

It was hard on her. For de Sales is known in Kerry

as The Football Nun. Poor de Sales didn't even get to attend her parents' funerals when they died within a few weeks of each other. So how then could she go to football matches?

Coming up to her eightieth year, she hasn't a wrinkle on her open face. De Sales' friend, Maria Ashe from Annascaul, explains why, in just three words. "Fun, faith and football."

There's a lovely innocence about her, here in the winter half-light at the noon of a bedraggled day when the trawlers are tied up at the quay of Dingle but still bobble like corks in the swell. The grand old cut-stone convent, known as The Diseart, shudders and shakes with every squall.

"Dara Cinnéide is my favourite player," she says. "He's such a gentleman." And then with the young girl's giggle, she sighs, "Ah Dara, my darling." But it's all just a bit of fun.

De Sales procured a miraculous Holy Medal "from an impeccable source", in Medjugorje, just a few days before the 2004 All-Ireland final. Dara was captain that year. Under strict instructions from de Sales, Bean Uí Cinnéide sewed the holy medal into her son's football shorts.

De Sales prayed all the way up to Croke Park and sang all the way home. Kerry won and Dara lifted Sam.

Then The Football Nun bounds up as if she's about to run for the ball. She acts a play from the day her nephew Johnny Horgan lost a county final with Feale Rangers. I was sitting near her back then. De Sales burst into tears at the final whistle.

The reverie is interrupted by the Angelus Bell. I'm embarrassed. I've forgotten most of the words but de Sales prompts gently. The Football Nun has as much time for the sinners as the virtuous.

There's so much more to her than football. De Sales works every hour God gives her. "Come on. I must look after the old people," she says, and I follow on. She's dressed in red for the Dingle team and de Sales walks as if she's marching behind the Artane Band.

We're given a lovely lunch at the Day Centre near the convent where the older people from all over the index finger of the Dingle Peninsula dine out. The sing-song at lunch time would lift your spirits. De Sales is older than most of the old people but she doesn't know that.

Their jobs are endless with the tending to the altar in Dingle church, collecting for charity, the minding of the housebound, and the listening. For a woman who talks so much, de Sales is a great listener.

But this is a sports column, sort of, and we only persuaded de Sales to talk if we concentrated on football. The real reason she agreed to an interview is my Auntie Kathleen was her mentor when the shy de Sales entered the convent.

"The Master of Novices said I was like a mouse inside a mouse hole, but I became a teacher and it was always in my head to coach football, but back in the old days it wasn't known for nuns to coach football."

She wasn't long getting over the shyness. Football was the spur, for de Sales knew All-Ireland senior finals are won in Babies Class.

"I used to let the children out to play in the yard and all I did was throw them a football and let them off. Well ...but my God... but they used to go at it hell for leather , until the bell, and sometimes if there was a great game going on I would forget to ring the bell."

Three All-Ireland senior medal winners she trained. Tommy Griffin was the first. Paul and Mikey Geaney won All-Irelands this year. Four more of her boys won minor medals this year.

De Sales ventures back and forth like a time traveller.

"Paddy Kennedy was my pin-up before I entered. He was captain in 1946 and I listened to the match with most of the parish on the Daly's radio.

"Paddy had lovely curly hair and I had a picture of him in my room at home. When we were eventually given our freedom, I was brought by my friends the Crowleys from Ardfert to a Kerry game in Killarney. I thought I'd burst with the excitement.

"Paddy was at the game he put his arm around my shoulders and well... I blushed. " There's another giggle, and do you know, didn't she blush again, 50 years on.

She has had her tough times too. De Sales fought back from a stroke and she says it was her prayers to God not to take her that saved her, as she had so much more work to do. There's a toughness there also and she doesn't give in.

We tour the convent. The Diseart chapel is home to RTE's 'Other Voices' and to the most exquisite Harry Clarke stained-glass windows. I look in admiration as a rare winter ray, filtered by Harry, lights up the crib and the Baby Jesus.

We ask de Sales if she would have liked to have had children of her own.

"But I had so many children," she laughs. And then it's as if she's transported back in time again. The Nun rocks her cradled arms over and back.

"My niece Suzanne gave me her little baby Olan to hold while she was out shopping. He went off to sleep there in my arms and there was just the two of us. Ah but Billy he was lovely, and I said my rosary as the baby Olan slept. It was the most beautiful hour I ever had in my life."

The tempest stills to an ordinary gale. I ask de Sales

to bring me to the nuns' cemetery in the grounds of the Diseart. A huge old copper beech covers the square grave. Her departed friends, the 75 sisters who lived and died here, are buried in neat rows under small white crosses, like you'd see in The Somme.

De Sales picks up a fallen leaf and shows me the space allotted to her. The last one in the nun's plot. Before thinking it through, I ask if she's afraid of death.

Natural

"No, not at all. Sure won't I be among friends? There's no need to be afraid. It's natural and just another part of our journey."

We stay a while to say a prayer. But you sense it's more than that. De Sales is chatting with her friends.

The Football Nun has no notion of going anywhere far away in the immediate future .

"I wouldn't mind staying around a while longer. There are still a few more All-Irelands to be won, if God spares me."

And talking all the time, the Last Nun of the Dingle Convent, links me out through the whispering spirits, and the loved-for gardens of her old stone home, to the Diseart car park.

The emigrant looked up at the glory of it all. And it was then it dawned on him that the very same moon was shining down in the place he loved best back home.

50

We Irish Need To Give Our New Neighbours The Chance To Make Their Case For Inclusion

December 12, 2016

THE emigrant told me of a Christmas night in New York when he was heartbroken for home. He was asked over for the traditional Christmas dinner by some friends and they had a lovely day.

The emigrant was heading off from Bainbridge Avenue in the Irish Bronx for upstate New York. He was lonely for home. It was the night of a full moon. Just like tonight.

The emigrant looked up at the glory of it all. And it was then it dawned on him that the very same moon was shining down in the place he loved best back home.

In his mind's eye he could see the stream he passed every day on his way to school and the sound of the gurgling waters slaloming in and out through the stones soothed his pain.

Most of the Blasket Islanders emigrated to Springfield and Hartford in Connecticut. The islanders had a tough life.

Fishing was the main source of food and many died at sea. When Meini Ní Dunshleibhe, the Blasket midwife, was an old lady, she said that if she had to live her life again she "would have chosen someone who was sleeping next to me at night".

THE VERY BEST OF BILLY KEANE

Women were up all night worrying and praying for their husbands and sons out at sea.

The women had to work too hard. The men worked to put food on the table. The women were fearful of losing their babies when they became pregnant if the weather was too bad for the doctor to come out to the island, even though Meini was a gifted midwife.

The islanders were a loving people. Family was everything and when the family left, the parents were heartbroken. Very few of the women were willing to endure the hardships their mothers suffered.

When the men left, the women followed. Quite simply, they had to leave to find a better life.

Their story is skilfully told by Michael de Mordha in 'An Island Community' and is brilliantly translated in to an Irish-English version by Gabriel Fitzmaurice.

The emigrants faced many challenges. My dad had to go to England for work.

There must be few Irish people who aren't separated from emigration by more than one degree of separation.

Two young girls who babysat for us came back in to our pub at Christmas two years ago. They hadn't been home from the United States for 15 years. It took that long to get the Green Cards.

The girls — whom I love dearly — were afraid of not being able to get back in to America if they came home without the paperwork. We all cried with the happiness. It was the best Christmas present ever.

The signs outside the boarding houses read: NO DOGS, NO IRISH, NO BLACKS. Dad and his cousin Denis Murphy had to pretend they were Welsh to get digs. They were caught out when Beryl the landlady noticed the two young men went off to Mass every Sunday.

Denis told me they were asked to leave. As Dad and Denis were walking away up the road, Beryl broke down crying.

She sent her husband, Henry, to bring back the two boys. Beryl and Henry, who were good people, looked behind the face.

Ahmed Lulu came to Kerry from Gaza. His story is one of many in the book 'Behind the Face'. Ahmed would never have left Gaza if there was peace there. His dad, Morwan, died of cancer just a few months ago and poor Ahmed was heartbroken.

He was trying to get his dad out of Gaza for one last visit to Ireland but it couldn't be done.

This lovely little book of humanity was put together by three remarkable women. Sinead Kelleher, Susan McElligott and Mary Carroll knew many emigrants who have come here from all over the world. Their mission is to tell the stories of real people. They are backed up by the Tralee International Resource Centre.

And would you be surprised if we told you that their stories mirror our own? Just black-out the names and stick in Murphy and O'Sullivan.

Change the place to Ballys and Lis this or Lis that.

I was so honoured to be asked to write the foreword. 'Behind the Face' is all about heart, bravery and love. There is so much ignorance and fear of our brothers and sisters.

The people who come here, like our Irish diaspora, try to stay in touch with their culture and the land where they were born. We must respect that love of their native place and the culture, customs and religions of their first home. Our country of emigrants must become a nursery for empathy.

Every pot needs stirring and we all need and every place needs an infusion of new blood to sustain and invigorate us. I love the new names of the new Irish. Galina Cotter lives in my mother's home parish and she was born in Russia. Hashim Al Hadeedy came here from Iraq when he was two. His father dragged the family back to Iraq and Hashim missed Ireland so much. He was an Irish kid who was totally overwhelmed by Iraq. Hashim came back home earlier this year when Isil took over his home place in war-ravaged Mosul. "Isil took the family home, the car, everything," Hashim wrote. "I remember when I landed in Ireland I couldn't stop crying.

"I just wanted to breathe as much as I could of the Irish air I used to breathe as a child, 23 years ago."

Welcome home, Hashim. I hope we haven't changed since you left.

We as people need to give our new neighbours the chance to make their case for inclusion.

Every Christmas we are asked to look in on our older folk. So necessary and so rewarding it is too, but this year I would ask you to look in on our new Irish.

Maybe some of you feel we should keep Ireland sealed off. All I ask is that you look behind the face.

Christmas is the story of a family who had to leave their home place. The mother and father were fearful their little fella would be murdered.

The foreigners had no one to stand up for them. Call in to the new neighbours. It's as easy as listening to their story. The onus is on us who have always lived here to make everyone welcome.

It might be a smile, or a kind word, or an invite for a cup of tea. We all need a place to call home, a place to love and live.

Take a look behind the face.

51

Welcome To Japan — Flush With The Finest Toilets And A Quiet Respect In The Land Of Whispers

September 21, 2019

Today's column is coming from Tokyo and the Rugby World Cup. In the last 24 hours we have made our way from Helsinki over the loneliness of Siberia, Mongolia, China and close enough to North Korea. The road works on the N11 were a challenge as was the M50. But we are here now in downtown Tokyo, with all the news.

The journey has taken its toll.

I'm typing this while sitting on a toilet seat in a huge city centre hotel with 2,000 rooms and a view of the city skyscrapers that makes Listowel's finest building seem no bigger than the pier of a gate.

The new cursed lightweight laptop only works in the bathroom, which is appropriate enough seeing as I have spent most of the day in a wide range of Tokyo toilets.

The Japanese are the friendliest people. I was allowed jump queues outside toilets. And this in a country where jumping queues is considered to be the height of bad manners. Their politeness is not forced. This is their way.

I am very sick from colitis. I knew I was bad when a young lad got up to give me his seat. The changing of the time zones is probably the main cause. Tokyo is eight hours ahead of Listowel. I haven't had a really bad attack for years. But we will battle on.

There's a positive side to everything.

The toilets of Tokyo are a wonder of the world. Nearly every toilet has touch buttons on the side. The one I have spent most time on has controls for a bidet setting, a shower inside the rim of the crater, a temperature gauge for heating the bowl, and warm air to dry the bottom after the wash. My beloved cousin Bill, who has lived here for many years, told me there was a bowl that analysed the stool samples and sent a report to the user.

Every toilet seems better than the next.

I did get out from toilets of Tokyo to survey some of the city. We are only here but a few hours at the time of writing.

The people will smile at you and say thanks when you make way on the underground,

The six o'clock trains were packed with people right to the edge of the doors which works wonderfully well even if it is very crowded at rush hour.

The commuters are wedged in to each other. But from what I could see no one was asked to back off. There is no aggression of any kind when the commuters vie for space. The locals fly around the place. Those of us from the country note that the pace is faster in Dublin. But Tokyo is home to the fastest walkers on earth.

One man was in a hurry for a train in Shibuya Station which is the second busiest in the world. He was going so fast he walked into a wall. And then he nearly crashed in to me. The man apologised before speeding off madly in all directions.

Shibuya pedestrian crossing is a very wide intersection which brings the people out of the train station in to the bustling shopping precinct of the same name. When the lights turn green hundreds upon hundreds of people come at you and they are all walking as if they've spent too much time in the pub on their wedding anniversary.

People make eye contact here and for such a busy city there is very little talk. The citizens of this city of 30 million are not loud people. The respect for others is the cornerstone.

The small boy was running about in the lobby of the hotel and he was. as small boys often do, letting a few shouts out of him. His Dad went shush. The boy kept on shouting. The Dad went shush again and the boy went quiet. The Dad bowed towards an older gent who was sitting opposite. The older man bowed back. The Dad was respecting the older man's silent space.

Personally I would have enjoyed the roaring boy more than the silence but we do talk too loud in Ireland. There is no roaring out 'aya boyas' here. This is the land of whispers.

Indeed in most of the places we visited the hum of the talk rises barely above the noise levels of a pub where sick men go to for a cure early in the morning.

The traffic is non stop though and quite a few of the commuters wear masks to keep out the fumes and bugs.

We were talking in our pub on Sunday night and one of the lads said when I walk in to a pub in Tokyo the locals will say, 'will ye look at the size of the people walking in the door'. The Japanese are small but the younger generation seem taller than those who came before them.

They will talk to you if you strike up a conversation. There is no wariness. The smiles are wide and real. I got the feeling the Japanese seek to avoid conflict which is not surprising when you consider their troubled history.

Very few were overweight. The people who milled in

and around Shibuka and Shinagawa train stations were neatly dressed. There were no beggars. Neither were there any lads in doorways selling weed and smoking same by way of advertising their product like a coffee shop brewing a fresh pot. Ireland and O'Connell Street please take note.

The shops in Shibuka have huge electricity bills. The Japanese have turned neon in to an art form. Huge screens turn night in to day and there was a huge queue for the opening of a new shop called GU. The money burns a hole in their pockets.

The Japanese women are most elegant and very dainty on their feet. The fashion for many is for long skirts with white socks and black shoes, which is almost like schoolgirl uniforms.

I have only been here a day but already there is that sense of a people trying to find the balance between modernity and the old ways.

The city is built around getting people in and out fast by train. Recently the Mayor of Tokyo apologised when the trains ran four minutes late.

52

Bravery Embodied By Women With Naked Ambition To Paint A Picture Of Rude Health

October 14, 2017

ANNA-MARIA QUIGLEY had never exposed her new chest to anyone. Anna had a double mastectomy and now she was sitting up topless at the counter of John B's drinking a shandy. The place where her breasts used to be was covered up by her hands. Anna was shaking and very timid.

I said to her: "If there's any problem you don't have to..." "No, I want to do this."

Anna travelled from Portrush in the North to be here for a publicity event in aid of baretocare.info, an Irish breast cancer charity.

The bar is quiet enough with just a couple of locals in for an evening drink.

Anna told me her story before she took off her clothes.

"My partner Jade died of ovarian cancer in 2008. I'm here for her tonight. I had breast cancer and a double mastectomy. I was diagnosed with a similar gene to the one Angelina Jolie has. It's called the BRCA2 faulty gene and one in 400 women has this. I was told it was a very high percentage that I would get ovarian cancer or a re-occurrence of breast cancer so I decided to have my ovaries removed."

Bex Toland is on her left and she is topless and voluptuous. Bex is 28. Siobhan Heapes is on Anna's right. Siobhan is 53, feisty and committed. Anna whispered: "I've never done this before."

I was going to hug her but wasn't sure if it was appropriate. The two girls put their arms around Anna. I have seen many acts of tenderness in this old pub and many signs of love but this was the finest expression ever. The three moved in near together as one, like a curtain closing.

Bex, the youngest, raised her arms, like a footballer lifting up the Sam Maguire, Anna laughed and slowly dropped her hands.

The plastic surgeon did a good job. Last week I wrote I had never seen a bad-looking woman. Anna is beautiful, feminine too, with a smile that melts hearts and changes old attitudes.

The photos were taken by David Hegarty and the plan was to get publicity but this was more than about getting the word out. This is about saving lives.

There are two body painting events organised by the breast cancer charity baretocare.info and they take place in November, in Dublin and Cork.

The girls slipped off the high stools and made their way upstairs for the painting. There was a single pink ribbon painted on their bare backs.

I got to thinking as they were being painted. Back when I was a boy the women used to come in here to our pub dressed in long black shawls. One man, Maurice Stack, who was over 80 when he told me the way it was, said: "Bill, if a man caught a glimpse of a woman's ankle in the old days, he'd be in a bother all day long."

These were cover-up-or-be-damned days. The history of Ireland was to be seen on the clotheslines at the backs of the houses in William Street where I grew up. There were the big pink and blue knickers which have been described by my Blarney friend Paddy O'Regan as "double gusset, interlocking passion killers, elasticated below the knee". There beside the big knickers, billowing in the breezes like a flotilla of sailing ships going in to a large harbour, were the smaller younger women's underwear, easily suspended and secured by just the one clothes peg. It was a tale of two knickers.

I give enough time for the undercoat to be applied and I go upstairs with Ken Hughes who is the event organiser. Ken is a retail genius and he was the one who came up with this idea along with another Corkonian Eimear Tierney, a writer and more fun than any woman ever. I lost five pounds in the last couple of weeks with the worry of it all. Sometimes I worry too much. It often feels like I'm a custodian of John B's rather than a bar man. What if it all goes wrong? What if some lad says something horrible to the girls?

Anyone can walk in to a pub and switch from seemingly decent to a lunatic in seconds. Some of my customers stayed away. One woman walked out when she heard what was going on. I didn't eat or sleep all week. I told as much to the girls and such was my state of mental disarray I prefaced my talk to our three models with: "I want to make a clean breast of this."

Up over the pub in our sitting room there were masterpieces unveiled before me in a room where my dad often read out scenes from his newly written plays for my mom.

It was a drama without any drama. The girls were calm and strong. The three artists came on a long journey. Thanks to Stephanie Power, Ruth McMorrow and Ciara Patricia Langan, who formed a bond with their human canvasses.

Anna had a soaring eagle painted on her front and she was copper coloured with red spiky hair. "Can anyone see me?"

On went extra layers of paint but already I could see she was changing before our very eyes. Anna was beginning to get in to her role like an actress about to go on stage.

Bex was good fun and told us of how she found freedom by taking off her clothes for the cause during a naked bike event.

All three women had terrible health problems and body issues. They spoke openly and honestly. I realised just how little I knew about what women go through just because they are women.

Back when I was young if a woman went in to hospital it was dismissed by the man as "women's troubles". But the girls were for everyone and in no way anti-men. Said Siobhan: "Men, too, must check themselves."

She said to herself and everyone else, like a captain trying to rally the troops before a big game: "You're a f***ing miracle."

None of my three girls up there in our sitting room would ever be able to have a baby. Women's troubles.

Bex gave a whoop. She had some journey and some story to tell but she's strong now.

The girls were getting ready to go downstairs and the bar was full.

Anna the Eagle, buoyed up by her new friends, said: "We are real women." And so they are.

When we were small my dad would sit us up in his lap and tell us stories here in our sitting room. He oft times postponed the end for another night.

If you are good, I will tell you more next week about a never-to-be-forgotten night in our pub.

In the meantime girls, check those breasts.

> **Lulu Fitz switched off her beloved Larry Gogan for a week before the game because he played a request for Jimmy Keaveney**

53

Smitten By Bare Knee In The Dublin Moonlight

August 4, 2001

THE first time I met Bare Knee was in the Baggot Inn the night before Kerry played Dublin in the All-Ireland football final of 1975.

She was shaking a tambourine in a rock band by the name of Lacca and the Daisicals. Her brother Lacca was the lead singer and the Daisicals were to be the next Thin Lizzy. The people around me were shaking their heads and playing imaginary guitars.

I was in shock. I couldn't even play a real guitar not to mind an imaginary one and was fully sure that if I shook my head as violently as Lacca, Bare Knee and the Daisicals I would be watching the All-Ireland in St Vincent's Hospital.

What puzzled me most was that there was no mention of the match. I couldn't understand it. There was talk of little else in Kerry. My grandmother Hannah did the nine Fridays in one day. Nora Hickey, who was my boss in John B's, painted the radio green and gold and her cat Elvis had a narrow escape from the paintbrush.

Lulu Fitz switched off her beloved Larry Gogan for a week before the game because he played a request for Jimmy Keaveney. "I do melt when I hears Larry Gogan on the radio," she announced, "but as much as I loves Larry, the Kingdom comes first."

The mothers of Kerry were particularly protective of that Kerry team, the youngest ever to leave the county. One woman even travelled from Tralee to Listowel to throw a bottle of Fatima water over Tim Kennelly.

The propaganda emanating from the Kerry camp suggested Kerry didn't care who won or lost once the kids came back safe. Mick O'Dwyer may not have studied psychology at Trinity, but he could buy and sell any of the esteemed professors up there.

Back at the Baggot Inn, I approached the beautiful percussionist. "I'm Billy. I'm up for the match."

"Hi Billy," she replied in a strong Dublin accent, "I'm Bare Knee. Who's in the match?"

I was amazed but delighted. I was sick of the Kerry girls going on about Johnno's legs and Mikey's smile. You see, in 1975 every one of the Kerry team was single. It was hard enough to keep up to them on the pitch, let alone on the dance floor.

Lacca, Bare Knee's brother, invited my two friends, the Sexton brothers, and your correspondent back to his house for a party. The brothers, who both played rugby for Ireland and were big strong boys, were slow to move.

They were a small bit afraid of going to a Dublin rock party, but I was besotted by Bare Knee so off we went. The Sexton boys told me afterwards that they thought the party would be full of lunatics smoking cigarettes that smelled of burning furze bushes.

To tell the truth, I was a little bit scared myself. I could picture the headlines: 'Kerryman drowns in rock star's swimming pool. Push in the back suspected'.

There was no need to worry. Lacca's mother supervised proceedings. The strongest drink available was tea and it came as a great shock to us Kerry boys that Dublin rock stars liked lightly buttered Marietta biscuits just as much as we did.

Only once was there a danger of disharmony. Mrs Lacca asked Jerry Sexton what he thought of the Daisicals. Jerry, who never tells lies, replied ambiguously that he never heard anything like them before.

His brother Willie, knowing well Jerry hated the music, saved the day when he volunteered that in his opinion the band were the seventh best he ever heard. "Only seventh?" asked a disappointed Mrs Lacca.

"Ah but," countered the future Garryowen, Munster and Irish star, "I'm including the Stones, the Beatles and the lads in that poll. And sure Thin Lizzy are only ninth."

Why did Willie use the number seven to describe the chart placing of the Dublin band? Well, it wasn't an accident. We had Mick Carey to thank for that.

Mick was the greatest football manager of them all. He coached us Listowel lads from the age of four to 40. His lovely way of pronouncing Highbury persuaded every small boy in town that Mick starred seven seasons with the Arsenal when he was in reality playing for McAlpine in far muddier stadia around North London.

Mick was a lovely man. He always brought me a present from England for Christmas and even named me Tibbles after his famous cat who used to teach Wren boys how to play the fiddle. Oh yes, number seven.

Mick always told us if we were ever telling a fib to use an odd number. For example, if you said you caught ten white trout nobody would believe you, but if you said 'I got 23 trout last night,' you'd have plenty of takers.

Anyway, the Sextons walked home from Ballymun that night while I travelled back to the Ormond Hotel in some style on the back of Bare Knee's Honda 50.

The moon was a big yellow football resting on the top of The Clarence Hotel on the other side of the river as we kissed goodbye on Ormond Quay.

There are some mighty moons around All-Ireland time. In other parts of the world they are called harvest moons, but in Kerry we call them All-Ireland moons. For a moment or two, I even forgot about the game.

The next morning in the dining room of the Ormond Hotel there was a hop ball from our local bookmaker Eric Browne: "Fair play to you," said Eric. "In Dublin only a day and you're courting rock stars."

The Ormond was something of a Kerry enclave in those days and a big cheer went up from the assembled diners. I pretended to be annoyed but, of course, I was secretly delighted.

The game. I'll never forget the tension. I had been the great Tim Kennelly's domestique at wing-back for the previous two seasons with Listowel. I played alongside Páidí Ó Sé when he captained St Michael's, Listowel to win the Kerry Colleges cup for the first time a few months previously.

Jimmy Deenihan and I travelled the country together. All three were great friends of mine and still are. I kicked every ball with them that day. In later years, the rest of that Kerry team became the most accessible sportsmen in the country, but in 1975 I only knew the three lads.

Kerry won, of course, and that was the start of the great rivalry with the Dubs which continues in Thurles today.

Back in '75, though, we Kerry boys thought all Dubs were chancers who lived on chips and Swiss rolls. Many Dubs thought Kerrymen were muck savages who ate nothing only spuds, half-cooked mackerel and the odd lost holidaymaker.

But in the years since then a special bond formed between the two counties and banished such notions forever. Listowel Races, for example, wouldn't be the same without Jimmy Keaveney, Paddy Cullen and their pals. Bernard Brogan, the hero of '77, married my next door neighbour, the lovely Marie Keane-Stack.

That scene in Bare Knee's kitchen has been replicated a thousand times all over Dublin on the nights before big games.

And still it goes on. A customer of our bar who, if he were an item for sale on a supermarket shelf would have been removed long ago, continues to have great notions of women.

"I have a date with a Dublin girl at the match on Saturday," he recently informed a fellow imbiber. "What's her name, where's she from and how did you meet her?" asked his drinking companion, Christy Sheehy, who should be snapped up immediately by the Tribunal Industry.

"Well, Christy she's from a place called Foxes Rock next door to Leopardstown Racecourse. We're doin' a bit of a line on the internet for the last few months and her name is www.ineedaman.com," replied www.listowel-lover.com earnestly. I hope it works out.

As for myself, I kept up contact with Bare Knee until she emigrated like many thousands of my generation in 1979. From time to time, Lacca would 'phone me when he was stuck for a new name for a band. Fig and the Rolls was one I came up with. Arachna and the Phobias was another.

My favourite though was White Pudding and the Flesh-eating Vegetarians. (Lacca was going through a punk phase at the time).

I even took to the stage for Bare Knee's farewell gig. I

just kept on shouting "I love pandy" every few minutes. One of the Daisicals asked me who Pandy was. Pandy, I explained, was not a person but a North Kerry word for lightly-seasoned mashed potato made with butter, onions and milk.

"That's cool man," replied the Daisical and he went back to screeching and bawling about "a preacher man who stole his baby". Apparently, a clerical student from All Hallows ran off with his girl a few weeks previously.

As for today, I think Kerry will just about get there. Dublin have improved dramatically from last year. They are voraciously hungry. It's going to be the most intense game of the year.

The Sextons and I will meet at a secret destination in Thurles for a pint before the game. Mick Carey won't be joining us. He died about 15 years ago. They buried him in the right half-forward position in Listowel graveyard beside the Listowel Emmets ground, Sheehy Park.

There's no better place for a football man to rest. Sometimes the odd wayward kick even ricochets off Celtic crosses and pebbled plots to the green patch that is the great character's final resting place. Mick and thousands of others will be cheering for Kerry in heaven today and that's why I think we'll scrape home by a couple of points.

As for Lacca, I met him in London last month in Bert Griffin's bar in Camden. The rock career didn't work out, but he has an even more glamorous job now. He's a train driver with the London Underground.

The years in London have knocked only a tiny bit of the edge from his Dublin accent. He's still the same old Lacca.

"Bernie is doin' very well in Australia. She's married with two kids now, she misses home though," added

Lacca sadly. "Who's Bernie," I asked him. "Should I know her?"

"My sister Bernie, you Kerry eejit."

Ever since that night in the Baggot Inn before the 1975 final I thought Bare Knee was a rock and roll handle like Sting or Bono, but Bare Knee is actually Bernie's baptismal name. You see 'Bernie' as pronounced in a Dublin accent sounds exactly like Bare Knee to us Kerrymen.

Ah sure, what of it. Won't she always be Bare Knee to me?

> **My dad John B Keane wrote 'The Field' back in 1965 as a warning over the "unappeasable greed for land". The trial of Patrick Quirke had much in common with both the play and the subsequent movie.**

54

The Tipperary Trial That Could Have Been Named — 'The Field 2'

May 2, 2019

PATRICK QUIRKE faces life in prison. Bobby Ryan was murdered. Lives are in ruins, there are no secrets — and all over a few fields. There have been many day-trippers who travelled to Dublin to attend the most talked-about show in town. The Tipperary murder trial could have been named 'The Field 2'.

My dad John B Keane wrote 'The Field' back in 1965 as a warning over the "unappeasable greed for land". The trial of Patrick Quirke had much in common with both the play and the subsequent movie.

My dad's mother Hanna and his uncle Mick Purtill fought in the War of Independence. The war was more than about independence. The Irish people wanted their land back.

My nana told me the story of how a baby and her mother were found dead outside the door of the work-house in Listowel on a cold January morning in the late 1840s. The baby was at her mother's breast, but there was no milk. The mother and baby had been evicted from their smallholding for non-payment of rent. This story was told to my nana by her mother, who was alive during the Famine.

People died for the land and fought for the land. The way of the land was "we will give you the shirt off our backs, but not the grass off our fields".

The prosecution in the Tipperary murder trial proved Bobby Ryan was murdered by Quirke because he was the boyfriend of Mary Lowry. Quirke was Mary's ex, and Quirke would lose out on the land he was renting from her.

Ms Justice Eileen Creedon, in her summing-up, referred to correspondence between solicitors about the termination of Quirke's lease on Ms Lowry's farm. No lease meant no Lowry land for Quirke.

Quirke owned 50 acres and rented 110 acres. He milked 100 cows. Where was he going to feed the cows? Fifty acres is a small enough holding nowadays. Quirke needed the Lowry land, and he needed it badly.

There is hardly a month goes by that there is not some mention of 'The Field' in the course of bitter disputes in the courts over land.

My dad saw and heard of many land disputes in our pub. He thought that by writing the play, he could show people the error of their ways. There was a bomb threat to the pub before 'The Field' was about to be produced. We lived over the bar, but my mother told my dad he had to write the play.

My mother was a farmer's daughter and she knew all about the poison spread by land disputes. Jim Sheridan and Richard Harris got that across brilliantly in the movie. Harris was nominated for best actor in the Academy Awards.

Nearly every land dispute involves intimidation and threats. People take sides and communities are split. Families are torn apart. Very often, the disputes became generational. If you inherited the farm, you inherited the hate.

There is also a sense the protagonists in these murder cases are bound not by the laws of Ireland, but by the law of the land. The green grass is green gold. This is an insatiable lust beyond ordinary madness.

No doubt now that the verdict has been delivered, there will be those on all sides who will breathe a sigh of relief and say "thank God that's all over". But it's never over.

'The Field' is based on the story of the murder of Mossy Moore in 1958 at Raemore, about 11km from Tralee. Dan Foley was the chief suspect.

He was never charged, but he was boycotted by his neighbours. Dan and his wife lived a lonely life. His brother Mick was disabled and he used to play the concertina for the neighbours, but no one came to hear Mick's tunes after the murder. There was an attempt to bomb the Foley house.

The Foley land was sold, but Dan's nephew John Foley bought back the overgrown fields a few years ago. John always maintains his uncle was innocent. The evidence was circumstantial at best. John is still angry and we will see how the story of the Foley fields plays out in a place where the past is still part of the present.

After a visit to the scene of the murder, we wrote "there's a terrible, atmospheric sadness in this forlorn spot where such terrible events occurred over half a century ago. It seeps under the skin. The very land is anaemic. No birdsong here in this bleak place or the sound of playing children. It's as if Mick's concertina is playing a requiem for the dead".

I wonder will Patrick Quirke's conscience trouble him when the lights go out in his prison cell tonight, and for many nights to come?

The craze for land will diminish with the years, and will the grey-faced old man in the lifer's cell come to say some day: "Was the killing of Bobby Ryan worth all this?"

55

Hannon Raises Liam To Lift The Weight Of 45 Years Off A County's Shoulders

August 20, 2018

IF God ever made anything better than the hurling, he kept it for himself. Limerick take Liam at last after another epic poem of a match. Limerick at long last.

It was a day when thousands watched the silver screen in the open air cinema that was the Gaelic Grounds. This was a thriller.

The Children of The Sorrows rejoiced and paid homage to every clash of every ash, to every thundering Treaty thud, to every wristy flick of every Limerick stick, to every puck and every point, to every block and every stop and every treasury of every one of their three golden goals.

This is our game from time immemorial. This year's hurling championship is probably the most memorable in a long time and the last 20 minutes of this one was the most exciting game ever played.

Out there on Limerick's home pitch, Joe Canning's late goal was greeted with a sound no louder than a nun's sigh in the cloisters of a silent order. You could see the look of abject terror in Limerick eyes. Was it to be the same old sad story, all over again?

But then Graeme Mulcahy scored what turned out to be the winning point. The wait is over, Limerick is whole again, reborn and renewed.

Limerick did it for Joan Ryan and the many like her. Joan was dressed in a lovely green knitted cardigan. She is every bit the lady with the smile and the heart of a young girl. Joan never missed the pilgrimage to an All-Ireland with her husband Patrick. He's a Treaty Sarsfield's man. Patrick isn't well but Joan came to the Gaelic Grounds for her man and for her county. She gives a great hug.

Anne Reilly kept her Limerick name for the day. Her three kids were green from top to bottom.

There was a lovely moment when Anne's husband put his arm around her just after the national anthem. As a Mayo man knows the pain only too well and so it was he minded Anne.

Their little boy slept through it all. The cheering for Mulcahy's goal could have raised the dead and those that were there began to believe they would get to see Limerick win a Liam before they died. And maybe the little dreaming boy was dreaming of Limerick winning an All-Ireland at last. Dreams really do come true.

There was a treaty broken in Limerick in 1691 and a giant stone bears testimony to the treachery. These loyal Limerick supporters were glued to the giant screen and glued together by an unbreakable bond. They kept their word. Today in Croke Park as well. And the team kept their side of the treaty of communion.

So many stories of the long wait. Before the movie of The All-Ireland final we met John Leahy who taught hurling in Causeway Comprehensive. John was drenched in Croke Park back in '73 when Limerick last lifted Liam, and he too was ticketless. "All I ever wanted for the last

45 years was for Limerick to win an All-Ireland. And failing that, Tipp to be beaten."

Hurling lifts us and tells us we are indeed a people who can be rightly proud of who we are.

The heroes of Galway and Limerick emptied out every drop of passions pledge in our holy place, where sacrifices are made out of limb and sinew, muscle and bone, for home and fatherland.

Canning kept his head and scored seemingly at will, while all around were hitting wides. Aidan Harte from Gort kept on giving. James Skehill threw himself in front of a flying sliotar. He took a bullet for Galway. The Tribesmen died like All-Ireland champions should. Like men.

There was a sense of a wild and untamed Ireland and even pagan Ireland in those last few minutes.

Yes there are referees and don'ts but hurling is about dos and derring-dos. For no other game can set us free from the conventions of conformity.

Last week, I met a young Kerry mother who was charged €50 to bring her 7-month-old baby in to the Galway game in Croke Park. I have involuntarily touched bellies with men with fat bellies on the way to my seat. These men and women with big handbags are a far greater risk to health and safety than a small baby. The good news was a Galway supporter gave the mother his own ticket for the baby.

This was a tax on motherhood but today was the greatest free show in Limerick since The Pope came here, back in 1979. Limerick City Council and Limerick GAA paid for all. They could easily have charged €20 a head but they didn't. There are some who never broke the treaty with their own people.

Limerick may not have corporate boxes or fancy

restaurants or duck a la feckin orange ,but it has a heart and today thousands of hearts pounded as one.

In 1973 a young Limerick team won the All-Ireland and as Eamonn Grimes lifted up the cup on a rainy September day, hardly anyone present could possibly have imagined two score and four years would scroll by without a Limerick win.

There are new heroes now but the heroes of '73 will never be forgotten either. Nickie Quaid's Dad rests happy in heaven tonight. His boy is the Stephen Cluxton of hurling. It was a day for old ghosts and new heroes.

Declan Hannon from sweet Adare, led from the front. Declan raised the Liam MacCarthy Cup over his head, and in so doing he lifted the weight of 45 years off a county's shoulders.

56

There's No Show Quite
Like The Joe Show

March 26, 2011

JOE NOLAN, the president of Bective Rangers Rugby Club, suffered a massive heart attack just a few minutes after the Ireland-Wales game. His friends watched helplessly as a young Irish doctor in a green jersey tried valiantly to revive him, but it was too late. Joe was beyond saving. He died where he fell — on a Cardiff pavement.

Joe's funeral mass took place in Sandymount last Tuesday. It was standing room only.

The dapper Joe would have loved that. He was a showman. As he was fond of saying, there's no show like a Joe show. There was never a funeral mass like this one.

I was fortunate enough to join his beloved Bective Rangers, the friendliest rugby club in the world. Joe spotted my potential immediately and picked me for the 3Ds, which is not a bra size but a social rugby outfit, far, far away from the first team.

Joe's players helped out at the Tuesday night bingo sessions. Our coach called the numbers.

The bingo sessions were a much-needed revenue source for our club, but Joe had another motive. He was hopelessly attracted to the older woman. Our president loved when he was slagged off about his love of the mature gal, or anything else for that matter.

His friends agree we should remember Joe Nolan with respect, but also as he really was.

Mick 'Sweat' Doyle told Joe's story from the altar. There was no script and no notes. I am going just on memory. Here's a slimmed down version of Sweat's speech.

"Joe's wife Eileen was 35 years older than him. Joe got to know Auntie, as he called her, when he was an apprentice in Arnotts. Auntie was the chief corsetiere and you had to have an appointment to get to see her.

"Joe was as faithful as he could manage. He was still calling the bingo and sometimes he left me call the last two games as he had to bring some old dear home for her 'cocoa'."

As Mick spoke I noticed a woman not far off the 'President's Letter' dry up her tears. I suppose she was under the impression she was the only one.

Mick had his audience in stitches. I could see Joe sitting up on his coffin, immaculately groomed in his green presidential blazer and the spotless white shirt with the club tie knotted as if by a sailor.

The grey pants were ironed by a steamroller and the black shoes shiny as his rosy cheeks. Loving every minute. His dancing eyes looking out for someone to be nice to.

Joe was a superb organiser, but on rare occasions The Joe Show went all wrong. His pal Mick tells it better than I ever could.

"Joe hired the Bishop Kearney High School Band from America to play in the clubhouse on St Patrick's Day. The 300-strong band filled Bective. Even Auntie couldn't fit in anymore.

"We listened to the band through the windows from 50 yards away on the dead-ball line. No one paid in. There was no room. The band cost three grand. But Joe redeemed himself by bringing Joe Locke to Bective and many more besides.

"Joe even organised to get himself a trial for the Leinster junior team. He wasn't a great player, but every time the ball came back, on either side, a shout went up from the ruck, 'Well played Joe Nolan. Good man Joe Nolan. Thank you Joe Nolan.'

"It was Joe himself who was doing all the shouting. Joe conned the selectors and was picked to play for Leinster."

Joe was a born salesman. Colleague Paul Deering spoke movingly of how kind Joe was to fellow salesmen with Rank Xerox who weren't doing too well. Joe would put leads their way. Rank Xerox picked up the tab in Bective for the funeral party, even though Joe had been retired for a good few years.

The front three pews were occupied by the Dollies. The Dollies were formed as a Golden Oldies team about 25 years ago but have yet to play a game. These men were Joe's long-time friends. His family really.

As you might have guessed, Joe didn't have any kids. Us youngsters were his children.

Money was for spending and he he'd never see you stuck. He was co-ordinator of all our big days. Joe was the manager of the U-6 team that Jonathan Sexton played on. Jonathan was there to say his goodbyes to his first coach.

Joe was a gentleman. He was unfailingly polite and he never cursed. If he did tell a few porkpies, like when he promised five players the full-back spot, it was only because he wanted everyone to love him.

Joe organised the kids' Christmas party every year since Santa was a boy. One year he ordered a donkey from Fossetts circus to bring in Santa.

The donkey pooed a poo as watery as prison gravy all over the Bective dancehall floor. Joe told the kids the donkey had a gallon of cod-liver oil for his breakfast.

Joe was never happier than when he was helping others. Mick swore Joe was on 'the make', though, when he started up the Donnybrook Glamorous Granny competition. We all laughed at the stand-up wake. It was as if Joe wasn't dead at all.

Then Mick broke down without warning and couldn't speak another word. Reality set in. But Mick did his friend proud.

I know he was going to thank Danny Parkinson, Joe's classmate, who organised the funeral. The Parkinsons were Joe's other family and looked after Joe like he was one of their own when he left boarding school. Good people to the very core.

Joe found true love again in these last few years. His wonderful partner, Rosemary, was by his side when he died in Cardiff. She got a terrible shock and had to be brought to the funeral in a wheelchair.

Joe hated sadness. I'd guess Joe had enough of that when he was a kid, even though he never spoke of his parents' death

Our president wouldn't have liked this to end up on a 'sorry for your troubles' note. Joe always wanted a happy ending.

I won't bullshit you with 'wasn't it a great way to go'. It wasn't.

Joe loved being president and it's such a pity he didn't live to see out his term. Besides, he had many more years in him as a civilian, but we'll obey his posthumous command. There was much more to him than the older women thing but here's his favourite story.

Joe was on one of his Rank Xerox reward trips to Florida with Auntie.

Auntie went off to warm up the bed. Joe strode up to the bar of the 11-star hotel for a double Smirnoff. This American lady, who was even older than Auntie, shuffled slowly up to the counter.

"Hey Big Boy," she said to Joe, "I'll double whatever she's paying you."

The visit cost millions and the money was well spent. Killarney is a wonder of the world. The message was sent to the British tourists that Ireland is safe, friendly, scenic and organised.

57

The Prince Knew I Was A Chancer, But He's Coming Back Anyway

June 16, 2018

THE Prince shook my hand. I think maybe he thought I was someone he knew but couldn't quite put a name on me. "I ducked over to see you," I said. "Ooh. You did," he said laughing conspiratorially like a schoolboy let in on a prank from a bold boy.

"You're so welcome" I said. "And who are you?" he asked, still laughing. I told him and he knew then we had never met before and I was a chancer.

"Will you come to Listowel?" I asked. "You'd love it."

"I will try to get there some time," he replied.

"Good luck," he said. And as The Prince was moving through the crowd, he said: "We had a great time and we will come back. They seem to like us here."

I'd say The Prince would love to go downtown and have a few pints. I was thinking of Freddy Mercury and 'I want to break free'.

Camilla, Duchess of Cornwall, came to our table.

"I love your green outfit. It's perfect for the day that's in it. I'm a writer and it's my job to give compliments to women, to women who deserve it."

"Thank you very much," she replied and she beamed a big smile. I did like her outfit. And the Duchess is a very nicely put together woman who looks much better up close than on TV. There was warmth about her.

The upshot of our chat was she agreed to come to Listowel for Writers' Week and I was given her card.

Across the way, I saw Sinn Féin TD Martin Ferris shaking hands with her husband. We met with Martin at the gates of Killarney House before the royals arrival.

"Will we get in?" he asked. "I'll get in Martin, but I'm not so sure about you."

Martin laughed and the former IRA man turned serious when I asked why he did agree to come here.

"I'm for anything that advances the peace process."

Prince Charles too has had to move on from the murder by the IRA of his uncle and godfather Lord Mountbatten, whom he loved dearly.

I thought of my grandmother Hannah Purtill, who fought for independence and suffered from post-traumatic stress as a result. And my grand uncle Mick who was involved in several fire fights when men were killed on both sides.

I think Nana and Uncle Mick would approve of my shaking hands with Prince Charles and Camilla. There will be no rattling of bones in coffins.

These are real people, flawed yes, yet wonderfully human too. The Prince and Duchess seem to me to be very much in love.

Every now and then he looked over at his wife and smiled. The Prince seemed to sense when Camilla need a lift after a particularly gruelling day. She always smiles back at him .

The visit cost millions and the money was well spent. Killarney is a wonder of the world. The message was sent to the British tourists that Ireland is safe, friendly, scenic and organised.

Where they lead others must follow, especially so in their own country where a blissful ignorance is rampant among many in government who act as if Ireland was far away and of no consequence.

The IRA is in sleep mode. It has not gone away. A hard Brexit border would be a disaster.

Charles and Camilla know us now. The next step is to persuade their people and their government to take us seriously, before it is too late.

So far as I know, this was the first time an Irish writer told the story of the abuse of kids whose dads weren't around to back them up. That was nearly 60 years before #metoo.

58

Record The Memories Of Your Elders — They Will Never Die If Their Stories Are Kept Alive

June 1, 2019

THIS old man came into our pub in the company of a matchmaker. The old man was a well-off farmer. The matchmaker was a bad man. My parents were wary.

They had cause to be. In came a young girl in her school uniform. She had been taken out of school that morning. I'm not quite sure who was supposed to be looking after her. My dad wrote his first play 'Sive' after that encounter in our pub.

The young girl never knew her father and her mother died. She was vulnerable. The Church and the government looked down on children born out of wedlock. They were sent off to mother and baby homes. As most of you know, they were treated like prisoners and thousands of the little babies died due to neglect.

Dad and Mam tried to stop the horrible match that was being made in our pub. The girl was legally old enough to marry. Her guardians were bought off and I am fairly certain the priest was well paid for solemnising the mismatch.

When Dad and Mam objected, the whole sordid business was moved on to another bar. Mam had Dad write about the story of the young girl. So far as I know, this was the first time an Irish writer told the story of the abuse of kids whose dads weren't around to back them up. That was nearly 60 years before #metoo.

One of the regrets is that I didn't put more time into asking Mam and Dad more about the history of the plays. My Mam's people had a country shop and I have many of the stories of the goings-on.

We are lucky in that Dad was on television so much. He was some performer. Mam didn't give any interviews until she was in the last few years of her life.

Anne Cassin, Deirdre Walsh, Ryan Tubridy, Mickey Mac Connell and Miriam O'Callaghan interviewed my Mam. Their archive is of the finest quality. Mam had hundreds of stories, though, and I'm sorry now I didn't film or tape her. I kind of hated asking her to do it then when she was dying. I know Mam wouldn't have minded. Her energy levels were low. I was afraid we would wear her out.

It's only lately that I have been able to look at my Dad on YouTube. I was too lonesome. I have had trouble dealing with grief. I'm writing this on the Thursday, and it is Dad's anniversary. He died in 2002 and the years have passed as quickly as if we were scrolling through an online calendar.

Nowadays I'm able to enjoy him. I give thanks for that. For a good many years, I had to run out of the room when he came on TV.

But now Dad puts me in good form as he did when he was living here with us up over our little pub. But it is one of the great regrets of my life that I didn't start filming or taping Mam in time.

A word of advice from a man who puts things off; get out the phone, or better again a good camera, and shoot the stories of the older people.

The younger generation could do the recording and so there would be a master class in life skills.

We are all the sum of the parts who came before us.

There could be a nationwide project with the aim of establishing a national archive based on the stories of parents and grandparents. The resource would be there forever for historians and the families of those who take part. Assistance in direction, sound and filming techniques should be offered.

The plan could be extended to the families of the Irish living abroad whose families would be made more aware of their Irishness and the keeping of their stories would lead to more visits to the homeland.

History is not just about big battles. The film makers would learn social history and how it is they are the way they are.

There would be life lessons and a shared experience between young and old.

We entertain a good many tour buses from CIÉ in our pub. You have to think of something new in pubs these days or the doors will close.

It's a constant source of worry to me. I'd hate to be the one who lost John B's.

I tell the Americans about 'Sive'. The Irish-Americans in particular have a passion for our history and culture. More so than many of our own who curiously enough are more immersed in American culture. I give it to them straight and tell the story of how it was the women used to come in to the little shop at the front of our pub, and tell their secrets to my Mam who was great to give advice.

I tell the Americans Dad was able to write funny about sad stories. There was the woman who told him she was expecting her 19th child. Dad was shocked. The woman was only skin and bone. "Ah sure John B," she said, "I love having the babies. It's the only holiday I get all year long."

I tell the Americans my Mam's mam died in childbirth. My nana had only four children but every time one of Mam's customers died after having a baby too many, a little bit of my mother died too. There was no contraception in Ireland and this was a death sentence passed by the Church and State.

The Americans are here for the real Ireland. I have never heard mention of a leprechaun. They too could be part of the project of recording the stories of our older people. There would be a massive tourism pay-off, but most of all, the struggles of their ancestors would be acknowledged.

The lawyer Robert Pierse is well in to his 80s and last week he published his autobiography. The story of an independent thinker is there forever now.

My favourite part is his mother's account of the burning of her home by the Tans and the British army. Robert's mother was only a child but she never forgot the night Woodfield was destroyed. Woodfield was the family home of Michael Collins, her uncle.

Many of the older people can see just how busy we all are and they do not want to impose. Go ask. My guess is those who came before us will only be too delighted to give an account of their lives and times. The story gathering could be done in small bits, and before long all the pieces will come together.

And if you think about it, our loved ones will never die as long as their story is told.

59

Noel Keeps The Green And Gold Flag Flying In Word And In Deed

June 17, 2019

NOEL O'CONNELL is a talker but his voice is too weak for the phone. He speaks in writing now. This is a talking column.

Noel has been sending us some of his life story over this past few weeks. His life's tenet is "I am a lucky man".

The people who are suffering from serious illness seem to find a special grace and gratitude.

Noel O'Connell was born in Cahersiveen, the town that hugs the mountain. There are few more beautiful places. His family left for New York in 1959 when Noel was five. There was no work at home, and no prospect of work. The boat was the only option.

The O'Connells made their American home in The Bronx , a thriving Irish neighbourhood, where there was back-up for the newly-arrived. Jobs would be found and a place to stay until the emigrants found their feet.

I'm reading Noel now — live. The words rush like the tide travelling up the Carhan River. He writes for the record and for the retention of the memory.

Noel can make that keyboard talk. I can hear the lilting cadences of his soft South Kerry accent as I read. He writes of his friends in America and in Kerry.

Memories "I grew up with these people, laughed and learned with them, cried occasionally and then we smiled and laughed again. All the time the growing continued, and the friends increased, all the time memories were created, mostly delightful, yet some were the painful sides of life that we all must face. And face them we did, knowing friends were in our corner when needed."

Noel's words are a homily for the Irish in America. This is how they survived and then thrived.

Even though Noel left home as a small boy, there is a loyalty to Kerry that transcends distance and time.

It is part of his growing up, the grown man, and part of his winding down. The strongest love of home is kept by those who have left home. Noel's people had to leave an Ireland that let them down, but there is no bitterness in him. Noel came to see us a few months ago. He was able to talk then.

I found it hard to believe that a man who left Cahersiveen as a small boy still had a strong South Kerry accent. It was the contact with the GAA that kept him Irish.

Here's Noel again.

"I had five older brothers who not only played football in NY, but hurled as well. I so enjoyed those days in Gaelic Park, meeting people from home and making new friends. Many of whom are still my closest friends to this day. The strongest bonds in my life outside of my family are my GAA companions. I relished those Sundays and my thoughts would always be centred on the men wearing the green and gold of Kerry. My family home oozed of green and gold, so my loyalties were fed to me from my infancy."

For Noel and many more, Gaelic Park was a few acres of home, an employment exchange and a dating agency.

We were boys at the same time. Pat Griffin was our favourite, along with the two Mick O's. That's O'Connell, and O'Dwyer. Noel's eyes were boy bright when he recalled the day Teddy Bowler gave him the Kerry jersey he wore against New York in the league final in Gaelic Park.

The Irish still come to New York without a job, or a place to stay. Noel helped solve both problems over a good many years. He trained the GAA teams in Rockland County.

My cousin Denis and his wife Anne told me Noel was always there for them in New York. Denis said: "Noel knew exactly what to do if there was a crisis. He knew where the cracks were and he knew how to fill them in. But most of all he was always in good form, no matter what."

There were times lately when I wondered if I had invested too much of my life in the love of my team and my place. Sports writers can turn cynical. We know too much about the bad goings on and maybe we fail to see good goings on right there before us.

When last we met, Noel whispered the stories of the big games, of the day he cheered for Kerry against New York when he was a kid in Gaelic Park. He told of 1975 when young Kerry played Dublin and had no chance of winning, but win we did. Noel was there. And he was there as we spoke. "This was the team of our times," he said.

My dad, who also emigrated, managed to make enough in England to get back home to Listowel. Noel's dad worked day and night to bring up his family in The Bronx. But here was a man who was more Kerry than I ever was and me only a few cic fadas from the football field.

"We were reared to be Kerry," he said in that last

speech. Noel, you were so right. Kerry we will always be. The soft fading voice there in the kitchen in the late evening renewed my vows. And I thought to myself that sport is valid and sport is worthwhile.

Noel moved to Pearl River in the 1990s. It's not that far from the Bronx. Pearl River is an Irish city, and the GAA is very strong there. The local Rockland County GAA club paid tribute to Noel last week. The hall was packed by his friends, and he has many. Noel was honoured by his own for all he did for his own, and for those he made his own. Every county was represented. His good works were universal and without frontiers.

Noel so loves his wife Eileen and their daughter Maeve. His girl competed in the World Irish dancing Championships only a few days ago. Maeve also played in goal for New York in the Féile. Noel was coach. Maeve and Eileen of the lovely smile mind Noel, enjoy him, and love him very, very much.

Every year, in the week before the Munster football final, Noel sends out all the news. He pledged today "to fight ALS to the fullest of my capabilities and then some." ALS is short for Motor Neurone Disease.

Noel's goal is to make it home to Croke Park in September "to see Kerry win the All-Ireland final".

I wouldn't put it past him one bit.

60

Worry Will Get Squatters' Rights In Your Head Unless You Embrace Every Moment And Live For Now

June 29, 2019

B E happy for this moment. This moment is your life.

I was people watching along the promenade of Salthill on Thursday last. The teenagers were jumping for fun in to the sea from the high diving board. School was out and the sun shone. There were hundreds of every age walking along the prom.

An older lady was helping her man. He must have had a stroke. She lovingly held his arm and brought him up along the prom. I thought to myself they must have often strode out when he was fit.

Maybe they had their first kiss here on the prom in Salthill, after a dance when they were teenagers.

I thought too of the way the lady has dedicated her life to minding her man. Judging by the slowness of his walk and his unsteady gait I got the impression the taking care of the stroke victim was a full-time job.

I was sad for them. For what might have been. I saw them in the long ago, when the two of them were as lively and as agile as the teenagers who were jumping in to the sea from the high diving board in Salthill.

I had no right to be sad. She was minding him.

The love was there. I was thinking of the couple before the stroke. That was then and this was now. They were in the now as they stood still for a while and looked out at the sfumato of Clare over the bay.

Be happy for this moment. For this moment is your life. The lines come from Omar Khayyam, a Persian philosopher.

I'm not sure if he meant his lines for the couple strolling oh so slowly along the prom in Salthill. Some say Omar may have been extolling the virtues of a youthful booze-up.

The way I read it was if you live each moment and work on that brief, tiny piece of time, then that moment will be fine.

This moment is your life and so is the next, and the next. The minding of the happy moments builds up in to a minute, and then an hour, to a day and a week, a month and a year, a life.

So how did the couple cope? On they went up the prom. The lady was focused solely on her man. He was holding on to her arm, for fear of falling. The two of them were taking care of each step.

This minding of the moments is new to me. There are times when I have terrible regrets for what has been and done. The worries come in like endless rain and they herd me to their pen.

I looked again over at the teenagers, jumping from the high diving board. It was the holidays, and the exams were over. Maybe in the years to come some of the sea jumpers might say these were the best days of our lives.

But I thought only of the moment when they sprung from the board. The teenage divers didn't roar or shriek with the delight or the fright. For those few seconds, they could think of nothing else but the flight. The worry about question whatever in the Leaving Cert was gone in the there and then. The moments of sheer exhilaration minded themselves.

All the world was shut out when they hit the water. That exact moment when the splash came is a place free of care. I have no notion of climbing up on the board. I am scared of heights.

There's no need to jump off a high board to find that state or place of minding small graces.

Take care of each moment. It's easier than trying to mind a whole life. You herd your own thoughts. Give a little whistle.

Just now, through the open window, I listen to the small birds singing in the big trees. I try to pick out each note.

I have this pal and he said to me one time I had a magpie mind. What he meant was I hop from one bright object to the next.

For the first time since I was a boy, I can pick out each separate trill from the tree-top symphony.

The green leaves shiver a little now in the breezes.

I haven't seen the leaves as individuals. It was as if the shimmering was all one picture like the pixels in the television and the birdsong was the soundtrack in a supermarket.

It is only when you pick out each note you hear the whole of the song and each leaf becomes the canopy.

I'm not saying we give up on work or whatever it is we have to do. Just pick out the pieces, and put each one together, one after the other until they join like train tracks.

Declan Coyle, the renowned psychologist and author of 'The Green Platform', advises we make a list of the tasks we need to do.

You make your own moments and place each task in order of importance.

You don't have to be careless to be care-free.

I was just going to write I wish I had figured out all this years ago. But that's not the way to think. It's about now.

My friend and IT man Bill Fayed from Syria is an Irishman as well.

Bill found a lost file of quotes on my old laptop. Be happy for this moment. For this moment is your life. These words jumped out at me from the hundreds of quotations I had collected over the years.

I have some way to go.

There are times when I let the worries and cares of the old days take over each of my precious moments.

In the end all we own is the space inside our heads and we should not part with that prime real estate lightly.

Worry and care will soon enough acquire squatters' rights, if we let them.

I tracked the couple along the prom. They crossed the busy road to the ice cream parlour in Salthill village. The traffic stopped.

The two sat outside, licking up the 99s. It was as if they were kids and this was the treat. A trickle of ice cream ran slowly down his jaw. She wiped it off gently.

They ate the rest of the cones then, tending to each lick, bit by bit. And the two of them were as one, happy out, in the summer sun.

61

Lazarus Rose Only Once, Mayo Do It Nearly Every Week

July 24, 2017

THE cast-aside footballers of Cork reclaimed the rebel within and Mayo as ever showed they are by some way the most resilient team that has ever played the game.

Lazarus only rose up the once. Mayo do it nearly every week.

There are days when we weep for Gaelic football but on Saturday night, in the atmospheric Gaelic Grounds of sporting Limerick, we were privileged to witness one of the best football games ever played.

Cork were a hurt team in search of healing. The hurlers are playing brilliantly and the footballers felt like castaways in their own county.

There's a courageous cussedness about the people of Cork. It's not in them to give in. Maybe it comes from the days when they took on the Tans and won. Or it could be Cork feast off the deeds of the great sports people of yesteryear in this the best per capita sporting place to be found in Ireland and maybe even in the world.

But I wonder who this Cork team were playing for on Saturday night? I doubt very much if it was their own county board. A lot of the big shots stayed at home to watch Tipp and Clare in the magnificent new stadium. Sad to say, but there were far more Cork supporters in Páirc Uí Chaoimh than in the Gaelic Grounds.

We salute the real Cork footballing people, and we met a few on Saturday evening. They have a team again.

We spoke to Billy Morgan, the Cluxton of his day. Billy said the worst part of getting beaten in Killarney was his Kerry friends were too embarrassed to slag him.

Well Bill, this is a team with a bright future, right here in the present. And so it was the baby who was left in the basket outside the door of the convent became the best one of them all.

The Cork manager, Peadar Healy, resigned immediately after the game. It seems to me you would want to be out of your mind to take over the managing of high-profile county team these days. Peadar wasn't paid a penny and he gave up two years of his life.

The minute a manager takes on a job, the sacking talk starts. The dehumanising sheep-worriers on the web would knock Christ for taking too long to die on the cross. You can go now Peadar with your head held high. The seed has been planted.

Mayo crossed several rivers and took over the Mackey Stand. Their desire for Sam is unrequited but their love of team is unconditional. The ratio of women to men was close on fifty-fifty. I have never seen so many women come out to support a team anywhere, ever.

This Mayo team haven't won an All-Ireland, and I would say, so what? Mayo have given so much glory to those loyal fans, so many memories and so many big days out.

There's succour too for all those who suffered from seemingly endless setbacks. Never giving up reaches out beyond sport.

There were so many 'stand up and be counted' per-formances. The two O'Connors kicked points all evening long. Aidan O'Shea was selfless. For a while this year he had the bashful look of a man who was afraid to look in the mirror for fear of being branded as vain. Aidan hit hard, covered ground and won the 30-70s, but it was his skill and decision-making that set him apart. He has to be in the mix for Footballer of the Year.

Andy Moran could turn the QE2 in a wash-hand basin. His kicking was of the highest quality. And his lay-offs were quicker than a bomb disposal expert.

David Clarke made the save of the year, and it's only mid-July. Cork sent in a high ball and one of the forwards got a touch. Clarke did an instinctive Fosbury flop from a standing start while at the same time finger tipping the ball over the bar. Who said men can't multi-task?

His miracle save was the loaves and fishes in reverse. The ball went over for a point and so it was the goalie turned three into one.

Cork fecked about for a while with the blight of lateral passing, but this game is alien to a county who thrive on having a cut. Cork and safety-first are a terrible fit. The ball was moved out of defence as if they were following a hearse going up a hill.

Mayo's tackling was relentless. It was at full tilt every time and they won scoring turnovers. Then the Rebels cut loose when all seemed lost. The big change was when Ruairi Deane came on. One of his solos was side-saddle and at speed. His mix of power, turn-tabling and skill opened up Mayo. The Bantry man banished the Cork blues.

Inspired by young Sean Powter, Cork ran at Mayo and scored two of the best goals you will ever see. Right at the end of normal time, Luke Connolly showed some nerve for a young lad when he kicked the equaliser after referee Ciaran Branagan brought the ball forward.

Cork seemed to have the force with them. Mayo huddled and worried in little groups.

An older Mayo lady, for whom every step up the stand was a Croagh Patrick on its own, seemed to be whispering Holy Marys to herself and Holy Mary. A youngster opposite us in green and red pursed his lips again and again, like a goldfish gasping for air in a bowl that hadn't been washed out for some time.

His fears seemed well founded. Cork started the extra-time the better. Evergreen Nemo man Paul Kerrigan, who had an almighty game, kicked a point and soon enough Cork were two up.

In a game where there many turning points, the one that mattered most was when Keith Higgins soloed up the field with a dash undiminished by the ravages of time, injury and mileage.

Mayo kicked on and after many twists, several turns, and a good few by-passes, they just about deserved the win. Mayo can't complain about the ref this time. Cork came out on the wrong end of a few close calls.

But the premature end, by 23 seconds, was a fair decision. Three minutes was far too long for extra-time, on top of extra-time. And anyway, Mayo had the ball.

Referee Branagan isn't easily fooled by diving forwards. The flow of the game was a testimony to his skill. He is a ref on the rise.

This was an evening to remember. There were errors and some poor play but Cork and Mayo gave us a game worthy of an All-Ireland final. Their story is for the retelling time and again, when games of yore, are recalled by football firesides, and small children's bedsides.

62

Listowel Hurts For Its Hero, The Horse

December 10, 2005

TUESDAY 3pm. I was driving out to Beale strand for a clear-the-head stroll when I saw the ambulance outside Timmy Kennelly's house.

"He's gone isn't he?" I asked Brian O'Brien, our teacher. Brian couldn't answer but his face told all. He just couldn't say the words. Tim 'The Horse' Kennelly, the unstoppable, unblockable, unrockable horse was felled by a massive heart attack.

September 1978. The Horse was a giant sea-rock between the Dublin storm and the Kerry goal. The water seemed to break up around him and spill away into waves as harmless as a puppy licking your toes. We won. I ran onto the pitch. I was the second to get to him; Hanahoe was the first. Embrace. The happiness in his face.

We often had rows but we were always close. Backed each other up. When I started out playing senior I was of an age when I wouldn't be allowed into a picture with French kissing in it. Tim was centre-back, I was his domestique at left-half. He warned me to get rid of the ball quickly.

Timmy knew I was so light that if I took a breath of

helium I would have been swept away to somewhere over the rainbow. Bang. Down I went like a sack of feathers.

The man who shouldered me hit the deck seconds afterwards. The Horse came in and blew him away as easily as a small boy blowing seeds from a dandelion. It was fair hit though, shoulder to shoulder, for that was The Horse's way.

Tuesday 4pm. There was a traffic jam building outside the house on the Ballylongford Road. The ambulance pulled out as Tim's son Noel arrived. It was sad to see a big, strong lad so utterly devastated. He was as polite as ever. Hugged and kissed before he went in to see his father. His sister Joanne, a lovely gentle girl, found her Dad. Noel was very nice to her; he has the gentle way of his mother.

September 2000. Noel is the first of the Golden Age offspring to win a senior All-Ireland. Tim is in tears. There is no greater honour for a Kerry father. P Ó Sé hops a ball. "Timmy, you're throwing great pups." I phoned Páidí just after Noel came in. "I have bad news, very bad," I told him. The phone went dead. The hardest man who ever laced a boot was devastated to the point of speechlessness.

Timmy and P Ó just loved each other's company. They told each other outrageous yarns and pretended to believe them. Jimmy Deenihan was next to be told.

1987. The count centre in the Ashe Memorial Hall in Tralee. Deenihan heads the poll and is elected to the Dáil for the first time. The Horse wore out several pairs of shoes canvassing for his old teammate. Deenihan is carried shoulder high but the man underneath him is buckling. The Horse takes over.

"I've been carrying you all my life, Greek," he says to Deenihan. Deenihan looks down and says "That's what horses are for."

Tuesday 4pm. The family were unable to contact Tim's wife, Nuala. She drove past Pat Whelan's shop in William Street in Listowel. A big wave and a smile for Pat. Her son Noel and Pat's son Maurice starred in the Emmets' total football win over Ballylongford last Sunday. Pat knew, but there was nothing he could do.

Nuala always backed Timmy 100 per cent, on and off the field. Timmy and herself were mad about each other and very seldom mad with each other. Nuala worked long hours when they owned a pub and still managed to raise three lovely kids.

October '05. Bonfires blazed even though Kerry lost. Tadhg was home as a hero. The first Irishman to win a Grand Final. Tadhg stood up beside his Dad on the back of Galvin's beer lorry. Tim was so proud. Tadhg, a gas man, was slagging with his pals as ever. "We should have brought Timmy down to The Square in a horse box but he picked a beer lorry."

Tuesday again. Tadhg would have to be told before the papers got to him. It had to be Noel. The two boys are very close and Noel said he couldn't do it. But he was bred to be brave, on and off the field.

Noel woke his brother in what was the middle of the night in Australia. Tadhg immediately set out to see his Dad.

The sadness and loneliness of right now. Belfast mourned George and we feel just the same way about Tim. Lovely Listowel is a town in shock. There is no chirping in the voices of the women at their shopping, just hushed whispers. Men feel our back-up is gone. Everyone loved Timmy but Timmy was not perfect and he knew he was not perfect and there were times when that realisation upset him.

For sure and certain, though, Tim Kennelly was a

good man and a compassionate man who had a word for everyone and never jangled his All-Ireland medals around in his pockets.

He was a man who hated to see anyone down and he was at his best when help was needed. And that assistance was always offered before it was asked for.

It was, I suppose, appropriate his heart gave out in the finish because he was all heart. That was the essence of the man but there was no way the heart of a lion could be sustained by the body of a man, even a man called The Horse.

Tim will go for his last drive with his great pal Eamonn O'Carroll, affectionately known as Ned the Dead. His coffin will be togged out in the green and gold of Kerry and the black and gold of the Emmets.

But every man, woman and child in North Kerry will drape his casket with their love for the Pegasus, the flying horse, that was Tim Kennelly.

The final whistle will sound around 12.30 today. You might stop at whatever you are doing around then and say a little prayer for Tim and his family. And for all of us who were lucky enough to know him.

63

Gig On The Bishop's Tomb
In Kildare Cathedral

September 26, 2016

J UST to warn you, before we go any further, there's sex
in this column. And 'women's troubles' too. We know
from past experience that some of you will take offence
— but don't go saying you weren't warned.

The campaign to bring back the sheela-na-gig is being
officially launched here today.

The piece is very much aimed at men but women
might like to read the content. I'm sure most women
are in no need of a body map. I was in a doctor's waiting
room one time and a man of my acquaintance was reading 'Woman's Way'. The man next to him was shocked.

"What are you reading that thing for?" he asked.

The reader replied: "I'm only looking at it because I'm
trying to figure out what the women are thinking." So,
ladies, read on.

Not a day goes by but that an intrepid expert with
more letters after his name than Newtownmountkenne-
dy isn't paddling waist-high in some remote Amazonian
backwater and peering into murky pools for a previously
undiscovered species of lizard or a new newt.

And astronauts have travelled the heavens. But no
one was searching for the clitoris and the womb was a

place of great mystery where any ailment of significance was peremptorily dismissed as 'woman's troubles'.

Men have a better understanding of the topography of the moon than the womb.

There's no sat-nav for the clitoris. "Take the next left and move a little to the right, no left, right again. Down a bit, up a bit. Leave the M1 at the next roundabout. Nearly there now. You're at the last junction. Will you stop, will you? You've passed it out. Go back. Go back outa dat. Travel back again to Junction 2, just above the labia. No it's the labia, I said, not the fibia."

Our guess is more than a good few men should have an L or an N plastered on their backs and fronts.

Last spring, we called on the Government to appoint a Minister for Sex. But there was no response. I often wonder if the only people in high places who read this column are either roofers or sherpas.

And it's not just sex, is it?

No man can properly claim to understand women unless he first learns how women function biologically and emotionally.

I was flicking through the channels the other night and I counted seven simultaneous food programmes. There were recipes for Moroccan chicken and Atlantic mussels but the only sex programmes were of writhing women trying to get men to phone them up at a very high rate per minute. We need a co-ordinated response and an Irish educational refit. And not just for kids but for adults too. The night class season starts around now. I couldn't find even one for men dealing with the inner sanctum of a woman's body.

When I was a very small boy, we had a snug at one end of our bar. The older women used to go in there for a secret sherry. The old ladies used to wear long black shawls right down to their ankles. Just in case men were tempted. I was an invisible boy. I used sit there in the snug listening to the old ladies going on about cystitis and thrush and no one took any notice of me.

There were men with 10 or 11 kids who knew far less about how women's bodies worked than the eight-year-old me.

I want men to know more. It's time then to bring back the sheela-na-gig or a modern version thereof.

The sheela-na-gig was a woman made of stone. And don't go saying your partner is one of them. Maybe if you knew more about her body then you would get a better response.

This definition is from Barbara Freitag's excellent book 'Sheela-na-gigs: Unravelling an Enigma': "Sheela-na-gigs are stone carvings of women exposing their genitalia."

There are sheelas all over Ireland. Many are to be found in medieval churches. The carvings are graphic, crude and even grotesque representations.

There is some controversy as to their origins and meaning but at least there was some sort of sex education going on centuries ago.

We haven't made much progress since.

Some of the sheelas were destroyed by embarrassed clergymen. Some are in the national museum.

And there's bound to be one in a church near you. Not in any modern church though, only in old ruins.

There seems to have been a conspiracy going on to keep the workings of a woman's body a state and church secret.

My theory is the sufferings of women were to be kept quiet in case there would be some sort of break in the birthing of Catholics. Doctors warned women if they had any more kids, then they would die.

And die they did. That's not a hundred years ago either. Contraception only became legal in Ireland in recent times.

So here is our proposal. We must bring back the shee-la-na-gig. Every man in Ireland should be given a free guided tour of the workings of a woman's body.

The tour can be virtual but I would suggest a life-size working model made in the best labs, a latter-day sheela with respect, technology and tactile responses.

There seems to be a terrible embarrassment when it comes to discussing sex education or "women's troubles" in this country.

Every home should own a sheela. Bring back sheela.

64

The Jersey Comes First In The Battle Between Husband And County

May 16, 2017

THE feed was banged on top of the table, without so much as a word. The new diet had caused some friction.

The dinner, if you could call it a dinner, was the young lad's favourite. The county team nutritionist gave his mother the recipe for hummus energy balls and a side of high-fibre fricassee of flaxseed fillet filled full of falafel and bagel.

The father of the county man was in a desperate state. There was a danger his belt might go around him twice.

The father grumbled, under his breath, but not enough as not to be heard. "This is no grub for a farmer. I'm a rabbit everywhere except in the bedroom."

He downed tools. "I can't take no more. All I wants is a feed of bacon and cabbage with real spuds and not dem orangey sweet potato wans either, but Aran Banners and Kerr Pinks, dripping with butter."

The thought of the traditional dinner Pavloved a slow slurry of saliva down the deep crevices of his once jowly jaw.

His missus was not for turning. She was a formidable woman. It was said the young lad got the bit of size from his mother's people.

The mother stood up to her full six feet and folded her arms by way of showing, through body language, that she was closed to any debate. She then placed a Wellington the size of a tuba on the chair next to where her husband was sitting, next to the untouched starter of couscous in a lemon drizzle.

The wife finally broke her silence. "Are you not proud to see your fine, strong, well fed-son on the county team? Don't you know he's on the county man's diet. It's all scientifically proven. The Dubs are on a protein shake made from camel's colostrum specially brought in from Morocco, and Cork are feasting on a plague of Saharan protein locusts."

"But," said the fallin'-away-to-nottin' father. "We are in Division 7B and we have no chance of winning the All-Ireland even if we feed them up with every superfood known to man. Our forwards wouldn't score in Lisdoonvarna and we didn't win a championship game since De Valera died."

The father was in full flow now.

"And how is it all the greats of long ago like Bernard Brogan Senior and Paddy Bawn Brosnan ate mate and spuds every day? Now woman, have the grace of God about you and bring me a mug of tae to take the taste of mulch out of my mouth."

There was no drawing back and the mother of the county man planted her elbows square to her husband's face on the kitchen table.

Then she breaks the final link with tradition. It was worse than Brexit.

"There's no tae today. Not a drop. Your son was told by the manager, he'd be no use without the ginger, apple and rhubarb smoothies. Sure isn't there aten and drinkin' in them? No more tae and that's the last word"

"No tae?" says the father. "Ah woman," he shouts out and jumps up from the table. "Tis the end of civilization."

And countered the wife. "His sports psychologist will be here at three for a visualisation session. Have a hundred ready."

The father is demented now. "Visualisation is it? Visualisation? Will you stop woman? The only visualisation we had in our day was when we had impure thoughts about young wans in short dresses."

By now the county man had become "your son".

"Your son didn't milk a cow since he was called in to the panel three years ago. With his naps, apps and abs, he's never here. I'm a slave and he's above in the bed snoring in the middle of the day and him not even having a hangover."

In comes the physio, another 70 euro, followed by the strength and conditioning coach, the chiropodist and the massage therapist. More dosh. It costs more to train a county man than a racehorse.

His wife relents ever so slightly when the money is paid over. "I'll do you a treat for the supper," she promises.

"Is it a big fry-up? With lashings of chips?" asks her husband, as his empty tummy gurgles a succession of harrowing burps and endless banshee windies.

"No," she says. "The fry-up might only tempt our son to go off the rails. I'm doing chia seed brownies to give him an energy boost before training, and before I forget, will you put a drop of diesel in the car for him. Our county has no money for expenses. And we must buy Maca powder. It is the food of The Gods , the food of the ancient Inca."

The husband stands and has one up on her, at last. "Sure woman, isn't it a well-known fact the Incas were killed off by the flu and the Spaniards? One sneeze and they were gonners."

They argue about the Maca powder, the demise of the Inca and he punches pilates in to the ground. The battle rages. There's no giving in. "I'm leaving," he says.

"There's the door," says she. The jersey comes first in the battle between husband and county.

Bluff called, the county man's father tucks into a feast of shoots and leaves but he stays put. Half the farm saved, but at what price? And they say the players make sacrifices.